Daughters of Palestine

DAUGHTERS OF PALESTINE

Leading Women of the
Palestinian National Movement

Amal Kawar

STATE UNIVERSITY OF NEW YORK PRESS

Published by
State University of New York Press, Albany

© 1996 State University of New York

For information, address State University of New York
Press, State University Plaza, Albany, N.Y., 12246

Production by Cathleen Collins
Marketing by Dana Yanulavich

Library of Congress Cataloging in Publication Data

Kawar, Amal, 1945–
    Daughters of Palestine : leading women of the Palestinian national
movement / Amal Kawar.
        p.   cm.
    Includes bibliographical references and index.
    ISBN 0–7914–2845–1 (alk. paper). — ISBN 0–7914–2846–X (pbk. :
alk. paper)
        1. Women in politics—Palestine.   2. Women, Palestinian Arab.
    3. Israel-Arab conflicts.   4. Munaẓẓamat al-Taḥr īr al-Filasṭīnīyah.
    I. Title.
    HQ1236.5.P19K39   1996
    305.42'095694—dc20   95–17014
                                                                          CIP

10 9 8 7 6 5 4 3 2 1

CONTENTS

FIGURES

PROLOGUE

The focus of this investigation is the institution of women's leadership and how it evolved in conjunction with developments in the history of the Palestinian struggle since the establishment of Israel in 1948. Among the many women in the Palestinian National Movement, perhaps the only one familiar to the general Western reader is Hanan Ashrawi, the spokesperson for the Palestinian delegation during the early 1990s talks between the Palestine Liberation Organization (PLO) and Israel. Since the Intifada, the Palestinian uprising in the Occupied Territories, which began in December 1987, Ashrawi accomplished an astonishing success in speaking for the Palestinian cause to the international media and in showing a Palestinian woman in a prominent political role.[1] (More recently, Suha, wife of PLO chairman Arafat, also gained recognition in the West through her appearances on American and European television news and talk programs.)

In the Palestinian community, the Palestinian woman most widely recognized and respected is Intissar al-Wazir, who for years headed the PLO's social welfare institution, the Families of the Martyrs foundation. Al-Wazir goes by the respectful title Um Jihad, as it is common in the Arab culture to title parents *um* (mother of) and *abu* (father of), followed by the name of their eldest son. In the Palestinian National Movement, these names were also used as *nom de guerre*, especially by those in Fateh (in Arabic, an acronym for the Palestinian Liberation Movement), the PLO's dominant faction.[2]

The first time I met Um Jihad, in 1990, she had been in the inner circle of Fateh for a quarter of a century by virtue of her political status as wife of Abu Jihad, one of the founders of the faction. Abu Jihad died in 1988, machine-gunned down by Israeli commandos at their home in Sidi Bu Si'eed, Tunisia, in an attack witnessed by Um Jihad and her adolescent daughter Hanan. Shortly after her husband's death, Um Jihad was elected as the only woman in Fateh's highest Central Committee. Um Jihad made a lifelong commitment to the Palestinian cause before the Palestinian movement erupted in the aftermath of the 1967 War; she was affiliated with Fateh even before her marriage, when she was in her late teens living in Gaza. Now, she is back in Gaza after the PLO moved there in the summer of 1994, in accordance with the Declaration of Principles signed by Israel and the PLO in Washington on September 13, 1993.

It is tempting to write about these famous women, but I shall instead spotlight the political history of the women's leadership in the Palestinian National Movement, its rise and evolution into its current structures, its contributions and accomplishments, and the problems and obstacles it faced. Prior to the rise of the Palestinian National Movement in the mid-1960s, women's involvement in politics was sporadic and occurred mainly during times of crisis. The women's societies tended to be social institutions in which charitable work was performed by volunteers from the Palestinian middle class. With the fall of the Ottoman rule in Palestine during World War I, the small, charity-oriented Palestinian women's movement joined the nationalist struggle, contributing food, clothing, nursing, and fund-raising. With each general strike, rebellion, and war the need for the women's help intensified, but women's work remained dedicated to relief. The nationalist-charitable women's movement flourished specifically in the aftermath of the 1967 Israeli occupation of the Palestinian East Jerusalem, West Bank and Gaza Strip (that will subsequently be referred to as "the Occupied Territories" or "the West Bank and Gaza Strip"). Throughout the history of the Palestinian charitable societies' movement, however, women's rights have always taken second place to the national cause. Concurrently, nationalism provided both men and women the sole context for political involvement.

The Palestinian National Movement offered the women's movement its first opportunity for mass mobilization, eventually reaching women who were not only from the cities but also from the villages—especially the refugee camps scattered in neighboring Arab countries and the Occupied Territories. Beginning in the mid-1960s, the women's charitable societies would coexist in a rather friendly relationship with a new, more openly politicized women's movement that sprung from the different factions that took up the struggle for Palestinian liberation. This book is an account of this historic mobilization that will focus on the women's leadership and its political organizations.

I first became interested in writing the book during the first year of the Intifada. Early accounts of the Intifada revealed that just below the surface of media-covered street events, the uprising was being sustained by an organized effort in which women played a vital part. The Intifada had initiated the third decade of the Palestinian National Movement, and it returned the liberation struggle to the West Bank and Gaza Strip; by then, the other arenas had become closed or restricted to Palestinian activism. At that time, I could not help but notice that at the top of the PLO only one woman, Um Jihad, was widely known. This book is inspired by the desire to discover who else might be there and to learn the nature of their work. There were a few available volumes, chapters, and articles that gave general overviews of women's participation in the Palestinian movement, which provided valuable sociological and journalistic insights. Invariably, however, each dealt with a particular period in the history of the Palestinian movement, mainly the Lebanese in the 1970s and the Intifada (see references). This book contributes to the literature a focus on the activities of the women's leadership by journeying with it over the full three decades of its existence.

My role, as a Palestinian, during the years since the Intifada has been limited to participating in bringing about increased communications between Palestinian-Americans and Jewish-Americans. Thus, I became part of a group of women leaders, activists, and academics from the two communities that met in a Dialogue Project from the spring of 1989, through the Gulf Crisis and War, and concluding with a visit to Israel and the Occupied Territories in January 1993. We met in the Dialogue Project about once a year and, I believe, succeeded in tearing down many of the barriers between the two groups of participants. Essentially, our purpose was concluded with the advent of the peace negotiations between the PLO and Israel, but we continued to publicly speak for peace.

The subject of this study, the Palestinian women's political leadership, consists of two groupings: those women who lived in the Palestinian diaspora and led the General Union of Palestinian women and those in the West Bank and Gaza Strip who led various women's organizations. The vast majority of the women are officially part of the PLO and its constituent factions, but a few maintain their leadership roles through well-known women's charitable societies. Most, however, are familiar only within their own organizations and local communities, and they are almost completely outside the limelight. All have been politically committed and involved in the national movement since their youth, yet their history has been largely unrecorded and unnoticed. It is with this realization that I set out to illuminate the collective experiences of these women from the early moments of their youth, when they first became drawn to public life.

To gather the material for this study, I audiotaped interviews with thirty-four of these leading women, plus a number of other women and men long active in the Palestinian movement (see the appendix for the full list and their organizational affiliations). Early introductions were made possible by a few crucial contacts I had; afterwards, the women I interviewed arranged for me to meet others. As a Palestinian-American and an academic, I was at once an insider and an outsider, but with each follow-up visit and conversation, trust and friendship deepened. In all instances, however, there was a certain ease that characterized my meetings with members of the Palestinian women's leadership, women who can only be described as gracious and generous in giving their time, often during very busy schedules.

With the exception of two women who left the leadership in the mid-1980s, the women I interviewed comprised almost all the top-ranking women in the current Palestinian political leadership. The vast majority of the women have been leaders for many years, and have been accepted and promoted by the male leadership. Most succeeded through commitment, sacrifice, and perseverance, but among those in Fateh, close relations to PLO leaders as wives and sisters was certainly helpful in attaining leadership.

In addition to women's organizations, the women's leadership roles extended to the PLO's legislative and executive institutions. Twenty-five of the thirty-four women were in the Palestine National Council, the PLO's legislative branch; the total female representation in 1991 was forty-three members. Four women were employed in the PLO's executive departments in Tunis and in Amman; this comprises practically the entire group of leading women in the PLO's political offices, which includes the Political Department, the Department of National Relations, and the Office of the General Commander (Chairman Yasser Arafat's office). The four women are in addition to Um Jihad, who has led the Families of the Martyrs foundation since the beginning.

The thirty-four women included the top-ranking women in each of the PLO's major factions, both in the diaspora and in the Occupied Territories. The number of factions in the Palestinian movement has always been in flux, but there are five that have had enduring women's groups: Fateh; the Popular Front for the Liberation of Palestine; the Democratic Front for the Liberation of Palestine (now split into the Democratic Front and the Palestinian Democratic Union Party); the Palestine Communist Party (now the Palestine People's Party), and the Arab Liberation Front, which is affiliated with the Iraqi Ba'ath Party. The women's organization of the Arab Liberation Front was strong, mainly in Iraq where there is a small Palestinian community but, in recent years there has been an increase in its activities in the Occupied Territories. The strength of the Palestine Communist Party, which only joined the PLO in 1987, is in the Occupied Territories. The remaining three groups—Fateh,

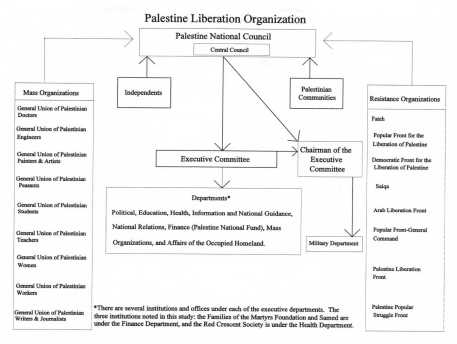

Figure P.1. Palestine Liberation Organization Chart

the Popular Front, and the Democratic Front—have had long histories of women's mobilizational organizations, dating back to the late 1960s and, therefore, they are emphasized in the narrative. Finally, since Fateh dominated the PLO's mass organizations, including the women's, its members comprise the largest contingent in this study.

The officers of the nationalist women's organizations are the core of the Palestinian women's leadership. Eleven of the women I interviewed were members of the fifteen-member secretariat of the Women's Union. This group represents women in the National Council and is the largest of the mass organizations in the PLO; the others are the students' and professional and workers' unions and syndicates. The Women's Union is essentially the umbrella of women's organizations or offices of the various PLO factions, but it also contains political independents (that is, people unaffiliated with the factions)—much like the constitution of the PLO Executive Committee. The main purposes of the Women's Union, as stated in its charter of 1965, are to participate in the Palestinian liberation effort and to represent women's interests in national and international forums.

The Women's Union was banned in the Occupied Territories from 1966 until the PLO and Israel made peace in the mid-1990s, and its place was taken by women's federations and charitable societies. Therefore, the thirty-four leaders include heads of the four women's federations active in the 1980s and early 1990s: the Union of Women's Action Committees, affiliated with the Democratic Front; the Palestinian Women's Committees of the Popular Front; the Working Women's Committees of the Palestine Communist Party; and the Social Work Committees of Fateh.

Generally, women in the charitable societies have held that their work was social and not political in nature. A few, however, have always been involved in the Palestinian political arena. The more politically visible group is represented here by three women who are known nationalists: Issam Abdel Hadi, who was a leader in the Arab Women's Union, a charitable society located in Nablus in the West Bank, before becoming head of the PLO Women's Union; Samiha Khalil, who presides over one of the Occupied Territories' most prominent charitable societies, In'ash al-Usra, and who is also head of the recently activated Women's Union branch of the West Bank; and Samira Abu Ghazaleh, who heads a society called the Palestinian Women's League, which is considered Egypt's branch of the Women's Union.

The Palestinian women's leadership is essentially a secular group, mirroring the PLO in its orientation, namely being nationalistic, pluralistic, and supportive of democracy. Of the thirty-four women (twenty-nine of whom were Muslim and the remainder Christian), almost all said they were not religious. The few who said they were explained that they practiced some of the rituals such as fasting during the month of Ramadan—but that they were not strict in their religious beliefs. Whether the secular character of the Palestinian nationalist leadership will change in the second half of the 1990s is currently a heated topic in the Palestinian community because of the strength of the Islamists in the Occupied Territories and the imperative that the nationalists come to terms with that reality.

Since the late 1980s, the Islamists have gained great strength concurrent with the eruption of the Intifada and the expansion of their political and social activism. Muslim women's organizations, for example, the Young Muslim Women's Association, operate dozens of kindergartens, centers for sewing, and other vocational training programs for women. Such Islamic social welfare enterprises operate outside the framework of the PLO and often compete with it. As of this writing, however, the political participation of Islamist women is still rather tentative and preliminary and is devoid of any openly political structure. Consequently, the Islamists have been excluded from this investigation.

My journey to interview the Palestinian women's leadership led me for several months during the period 1990–1991 to the Occupied Territories—Jordan, Tunisia, Egypt, Syria, and the United Kingdom. The

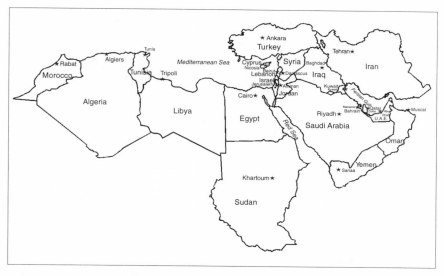

Figure P.2. The Middle East and North Africa

audiotaped sessions were held in a variety of settings: the PLO's headquarters in Tunis, the offices of the Popular Front for the Liberation of Palestine and the Democratic Front for the Liberation of Palestine, the Yarmuk refugee camp in Syria, the Democratic Front's Jordanian People's Party headquarters in Amman, the former Arab League headquarters in Tunis, and in private homes. The Egyptian interviews were mostly taped at *beit al-talibat*, a boarding house for Palestinian women students (on the rooftop balcony against the background sounds of downtown Cairo).

During the same period, I also had conversations with several of the top leaders in the PLO and a number of female and male active members. On various occasions between 1990 and 1994, I renewed contact with several of the women leaders, during my visits to the Middle East, by telephone and through correspondence. These communications proved invaluable in updating my information gained from the taped interviews and from my survey of the literature on the Palestinian movement and the participation of the women in it.

The book offers five chapters and an epilogue. Chapter 1, "Three Generations of Women," contains social and political background information on the thirty-four women. It emphasizes political events during the period 1948–1967, which acted as crucial catalysts of these leaders' lifelong commitment to the Palestinian cause. Chapters 2–5, "Amman," "Beirut," "Tunis," and "Jerusalem," analyze, period by period, women's mobilization in the history of the Palestinian National Movement, as its

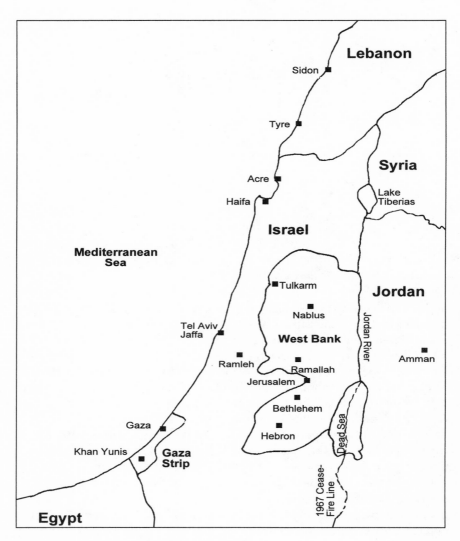

Figure P.3. The West Bank and Gaza Strip

locus moves from Jordan to Lebanon to Tunisia and, finally, to the Occupied Territories. The epilogue brings the narrative to a conclusion as the Palestinian struggle for statehood moves into the latter part of the 1990s. Indeed, the running theme of this book is the interplay between the Palestinian women's leadership and the surrounding political environment in which the women live and work.

ACKNOWLEDGMENTS

I would like to thank Mr. and Mrs. George Kawar in Amman, Jordan; Mr. and Mrs. Fuad Shehadeh in Ramallah, West Bank; and Mrs. Sha'ath in Cairo, Egypt for opening their homes to me and for their generous hospitality. I would also like to thank Laila Jammal, Samira Kawar, and Alya Shawa for providing crucial contacts for my interviews with Palestinian activists and leaders. I would like to express my appreciation to Ya'acub Dawani, Nazih al-Rashid, and Randy Simmons for reviewing several chapters of this book.

I especially would like to thank Barbara Nelson for her many hours spent reviewing the final draft of this book and for her invaluable insights. Her moral support gave me the courage to continue writing and also to enjoy the process.

I am grateful to the American Council of Learned Societies for giving me partial funding for the research through its grants-in-aid program and to the Utah State University's Political Science Department and Gender Research Institute for their institutional support.

Chapter 1

THREE GENERATIONS OF WOMEN LEADERS

I.

A remark Eisheh Odeh made at the end of our interview in 1991 best sums this background portrait of the Palestinian women's leadership. Odeh's history of involvement and her credentials in the Palestinian National Movement are impeccable. She is a former freedom fighter who had spent ten years in Israeli prison and had earned a seat in the Political Bureau of the Democratic Front for the Liberation of Palestine. She is also among the few women in the Palestinian movement who are considered bona fide "heroes of the revolution."[1] Odeh, however, came across as self-effacing, but it was from humility not lack of confidence. Odeh was responding to my statement that I thought of the Palestinian women's leadership as "daughters of the PLO."

What drew me to the word "daughters" was its strong sound in English and its common usage in works about women in nationalist and revolutionary movements—as in the study of Nicaraguan women, *Daughters of Sandino*, by Margaret Randall, and in the work about Indian women, *Daughters of Independence*, by Joanna Liddle and Rama Joshi; and, of course, Daughters of the American Revolution, referring to female descendants of people who participated in the revolution against British colonialism. Odeh had crisply informed me that "daughters of the PLO" was not a suitable term and her eyes expected me to know why. I didn't at the time. Not until sifting through the details I had collected about the early history of these thirty-four women did I grasp what Odeh had meant.

In Arabic, the word daughter or *bent* readily recalls its meanings: "belonging to" or "being given birth to." Calling these women "daughters

1

of the PLO," however, did not reflect the fact that, except for the very youngest, nationalist awakening was rooted in their youth during turbulent and fateful events in modern Palestinian and Arab history—long before the PLO existed. Thus, I chose the name *Daughters of Palestine.*

The Palestinian women's leadership belongs to three generations, separated not by precise age intervals but by the fact that their early political socialization was formed in separate but connected political eras. These eras include: the time of crisis in Palestine in 1948 that culminated with the establishment of the Jewish state, Israel, and the Palestinian catastrophe; the Arab nationalist period, from the mid-1950s to the mid-1960s, when President Jamal Abdel Nasser of Egypt led the Palestinian cause; and, the 1967 War that ended with the victory of Israel over its bordering Arab states.

The first generation is represented by four women born in the 1920s in Palestine, who therefore were young adults in 1948. This group, sometimes referred to as the "mothers' generation" by the younger set, became leaders via their work in women's charitable societies.

During the period 1964–1968, the first generation of leaders established the General Union of Palestinian Women, under the auspices of the PLO. It was a historic move because it opened up opportunities for women to participate in the struggle for national liberation, side by side with men. The first generation bore the memories of the Palestinian tragedy but, in the end, could only act as caregivers, helping those less fortunate. It was the kind of community work suited to their middle- and upper-class social background.

The second generation is the largest in the leadership, twenty women born during the 1930s and 1940s, almost all in Palestine. They became politicized during the height of the Arab nationalist and leftist movements, when Nasser of Egypt was the unmatched voice of the Arab world. The Palestinian National Movement brought this generation to leadership, and they were all members of cadre organizations of PLO factions. Their legacy was to transform the General Union of Palestinian Women into a mobilizational organization which, for the first time, included thousands of women living in refugee camps. This task was accomplished during the movement's Lebanon period, 1971–1982. Several women in this generation, however, did not achieve leadership status until the '80s.

The third generation consists of ten women born in the 1950s; about half live in the West Bank; the rest live across the border in Arab countries. (Together, the vast majority of the thirty-four women was born within the boundaries of pre-1948 Palestine.) The crucial political catalyst for the youngest generation was the 1967 Israeli occupation of the West Bank and Gaza Strip, previously held by Jordan and Egypt respectively.

The third generation rose to leadership roles in the '80s—and their story continues to unfold. Seven followed in their older sisters' footsteps as leaders of women's organizations, including the Women's Union in Tunis and the four unions of women's committees in the Occupied Territories. The remaining three worked as high-level political advisors and strategists, primarily in the international relations arena at the PLO's headquarters in Tunis.

Two in the second generation have served as advisors to Yasser Arafat, the PLO chairman. One is Sulafa Hijawi, whose previous experience included founding and operating the Iraqi branches of the PLO's Women's and Writers' unions. The other is the well-known face on American television screens, Hanan Ashrawi, who was advisor to Arafat during preparations for the Israeli-PLO accords.

Ashrawi is unique among the younger generations, in that she had not come out of either the factional ranks or the Women's Union. She had spent much of the '70s and '80s in private life, pursuing her education in Lebanon and the United States and an academic career at Birzeit University in the West Bank, only breaking out into public life during the Intifada, the 1987 uprising in the Occupied Territories. Ashrawi's prominence lies in her ability to speak for the Palestinian cause to Western audiences. As the peace process began in 1990, her impressive communication skills were drawn upon by PLO Chairman Yasser Arafat, who brought her into the Middle East peace process as a behind-the-scenes negotiator and spokeswoman for the Palestinian delegation at the Middle East Peace Conference.

Ashrawi's international role was an important breakthrough in the long journey of Palestinian women toward public life. It was a process that began early in the twentieth century with the foremothers who started the women's societies' movement, and it was intractably bound to the national quest for independence.

II.

For much of the twentieth century, Palestinian women who took interest in public affairs were from the more privileged families of the middle and upper classes. This early leadership approached the women's question with a combination of liberal beliefs in equality of rights and a deep sense of duty to volunteer. Several local community and religious-based charitable societies were formed (the first, according to Laila Jammal, were the "Orthodox" societies established by women from the Greek Orthodox Church in Acre in 1904 and in Jerusalem in 1906).[2] Notwithstanding, superimposed over a belief in social change was the years of foreign occupation. In the collective memory of the Palestinian women's leadership, the national question was never separated from the woman's question.

In the Palestinian political culture, the national tragedy began to unfold during World War I, promising the break up of old tyrannies but also shutting the gate of self-determination before it ever opened. During the war, Palestine became dominated by Britain, which then went on to rule it as a British mandate during the period 1920–1947—known colloquially as "the days of the English." European interests in the Middle East had taken an unmistakable shape during World War I, as the Ottoman Empire, which governed the region, saw its last days. The division of spoils was formalized by the Sykes-Picot Agreement of 1916, which set up British and French spheres of influence in much of the Middle East. It was formalized in the Treaty of Paris, which established the mandate system, thus extending international legality to de facto British control of Palestine.[3]

The other document Palestinians considered detrimental to their liberation was Britain's Balfour Declaration (1917), which promised Jews from around the world a home in Palestine. It also said: "Nothing shall be done which may prejudice the civil and religious rights of existing non-Jewish communities in Palestine." The Palestinians never trusted this promise of protection and instead saw the declaration as a clear sign of British betrayal of their aspirations for independence.

At the time of the Balfour Declaration, the Jewish population in Palestine was still a small minority; they were approximately one-sixth of the population and lived mainly in Jerusalem. But waves of immigrants were arriving from Europe through the effort of the Zionist Movement that rose at the end of the ninteeenth century, in part, as a response to nation-building in Europe and, in part, as a response to anti-Jewish sentiment. The conflict between the Arab majority and the growing Jewish population—and between both and the British—simmered throughout the 1930s and 1940s, and increasingly boiled over into violence.

The Palestinian community was weak and disunited. Their leadership came from notable families like the Husaynis, Nashashibis, 'Alamis, Abdel Hadis, and Shehadehs. Men from these families established the first Arab Palestinian political parties like the Palestine Arab Party, the National Defense Party, and the Independence Party. These were early signs of indigenous democratic development, and they were as much the manifestation of the debate over the future of Palestine as they were of traditional rivalries among these leading families.

In the end, even with military help from some of the neighboring Arab countries, the Arabs proved no match for the more resourceful and better-organized Zionist forces. The result was that the state of Israel was successfully established after Britain terminated its mandate in 1947 and turned over the responsibility for Palestine to the United Nations.

The earliest political stirring by women during the pre-1948 period was during the 1920s, when the leadership of the women's charitable societies movement began to grabble with the reality of British rule and with the increasing Jewish immigration from Europe. Its first collective action was in 1929, when leading women from the charitable societies convened the First Arab Women's Congress to voice women's support to the national cause.

The participants of the Congress made history by staging the first Palestinian Arab women's march. It was a remarkable procession of some eighty cars that travelled to the office of the British High Commissioner. There the women submitted petitions that demanded the annulment of the Balfour Declaration, the cessation of Jewish immigration to Palestine, and the end of the torture of Arab political prisoners.[4]

On occasion, women participated in political education by giving lectures or speeches, or writing in the newspapers about the political situation and women's issues.[5] Otherwise, women poured their nationalist energies into assisting families of political prisoners and martyrs and the poor in general. In the charitable societies sphere, however, communalism and the absence of mobilizational strategies for the masses prevailed, as it did in the political parties movement.

The critical role of women in social relief is of course a worldwide phenomenon, but among Palestinians it grew in volume with each new crisis: the 1929 and 1936 Palestinian rebellions; the Arab-Israeli wars in 1948, 1956, 1967, and 1973; the Jordanian and Lebanese civil wars; and the Intifada in the Occupied Territories. Charitable work, however, was traditionally perceived as a non-political enterprise. Posing no threat to the social and political power structures, it was safe for women in the middle class.

What distinguished the Palestinian women's leadership from their foremothers was its redefinition of what was political. The first generation brought forth the earliest examples of breaking out of the strictly charitable work, and they, along with the younger two generations, became new models for how Palestinian women could participate in nationalist politics.

III.

The turning point for the first generation was the year 1948, when the Palestine question became "the problem" or *al-qadiya*. It is also called the Catastrophe or *al-naqba*. In just a few months, the bulk of Palestine's Arab population had either fled in fear or were expelled by the Jewish forces from their homes, schools, farms, and businesses, and were forced to march to safety across the nearest borders to Lebanon, Syria, Egypt, and Trans-Jordan, as Jordan was called prior to 1949. Some took refuge in the outskirts of neighboring Arab cities like Sidon, Tyre, Beirut, Damascus, Cairo, and Amman. During the period 1949–1950, according to the United Nations Relief and Works Agency for Palestine Refugees (UNRWA), 726,000 Palestinians registered as refugees. (For the current refugee population registered with UNRWA and their locations, see table 1.1). First-generation women Salwa Abu Khadra and Samira Abu Ghazaleh were among these refugees.

Salwa Abu Khadra was nineteen when she fled with her family to Damascus from Jaffa, the Mediterranean city made famous by its oranges. (The 1990–1991 Gulf War was *déjà vu* for Abu Khadra, as she again became a refugee, fleeing her Kuwaiti home of many years and taking refuge at her daughter's home in Egypt.) In her '30s, Abu Khadra became one of the first female cadres of Fateh and later became general secretary of the Women's Union.

Samira Abu Ghazaleh is founder and president of the Palestinian Women's League, a society in Cairo that is considered the Women's Union branch in Egypt. Abu Ghazaleh was attending secondary school in Ramleh, near Jaffa, when she had to leave. Living first in Jordan and then in Egypt, she poured her political energies into charitable work. But the depth of her anger was transparent in a line of a poem she wrote in 1948. She recalled it during our interview in Cairo and it said: "Make me a soldier, make me a soldier."

Others found safety inside Palestinian territory, behind Jordanian and Egyptian army lines, later set by cease-fire and armistice agreements in 1949. This group became refugees in their own country, living in camps difficult to miss, near every Palestinian city in the West Bank and Gaza Strip.

Until 1967, Palestinians living in these two regions were put in the unenviable place of being close to their former homes (standing on a hill at night, one could see the lights in the villages and towns), but prohibited from crossing back. Those refugees who settled in Gaza and in the other Arab countries, for the most part, became stateless. Those in the West Bank and the East Bank—forming in 1949 the Hashemite Kingdom of Jordan—received Jordanian citizenship. In 1948, Issam Abdel Hadi, who lived in Nablus in the West Bank, found herself under Jordanian rule.

Abdel Hadi, longtime president of the Women's Union, was educated at the Friends Girls School in Ramallah and had hoped to attend the American University in Beirut, when her plans were swept away by the

Table 1.1. Distribution of UNWRA Registered Palestinian Refugees*

Field	1950 Registered Population	1994 Registered Population	Number of Camps	Total Camp Population	Registered Persons Not in Camps	Percentage of Population Not in Camps
Lebanon	127,600	338,290	12	175,426	162,864	48.14
Syrian Arab Republic	82,194	327,288	10	91,476	235,812	72.05
Jordan	506,200	1,193,539	10	244,026	949,513	79.55
West Bank	—	504,070	19	129,727	374,343	74.26
Gaza Strip	198,227	643,600	8	350,620	292,980	45.52
Total	914,221**	3,006,787	59	991,275	2,015,512	67.03

Source: Report of the Commissioner-General of the United Nations Relief and Works Agency for Palestine Refugees in the Near East, July 1, 1993 through June 30, 1994.

*Note: These statistics are based on UNRWA's registration records, which are updated annually. The number of registered refugees present in the Agency's area of operations, however, is almost certainly less than the population recorded.

**This total excluded 45,800 persons receiving relief in Israel, who were the responsibility of UNRWA until June 1952.

war. Afterwards, she immersed herself in charitable work and, in 1949, while still a young bride of nineteen, she was elected secretary of the Arab Women's Union. (This is Nablus's most active society whose projects include a children's hospital, a home for the blind, an orphanage "for daughters of the martyrs," and a secondary school.) In 1965, Abdel Hadi departed from strictly charitable work to help create the Women's Union—and was elected its president (this will be discussed further in chapter 2).

Only 170,000 Palestinian Arabs, about one-fifth of the Arab population, remained behind in the newly created Israel. My family was among those who had not fled by the time Acre, my hometown on the Mediterranean coast, fell to the Israelis. This Palestinian fragment was eventually given Israeli papers that proclaimed they were Arab citizens of Israel.

Regardless of the social, economic, or political circumstances, the Catastrophe of 1948 had the uniform impact of deepening Palestinian identity. Whether living under Israeli rule or in the Arab states, like the Jews, Palestinian Arabs felt rooted in Palestine. The Palestinians often revealed this attachment to their home surroundings by displaying traditional cross-stitched embroidered cushions, engraved brass and copper trays, and miniature olive wood camels made in the Jerusalem area.

In 1990, some 15 percent of the Palestinian people still lived in refugee camps, the vast majority of them housed in some sixty camps assisted by UNRWA (the number of camps fluctuated slightly over the years). Created in 1949 by the United Nations General Assembly, UNRWA provided aid mostly in the form of food rations, medical clinics, and elementary and preparatory education (and sometimes also payed for secondary education). Walking down the narrow roads of any of these refugee camps today reminds one that it was the former peasants and the poor who were left living there. It was the youth of this segment of the Palestinian population who, in 1967, were galvanized by the armed factions and their call to join the Palestinian National Movement.[6]

Predominantly illiterate and living on owned or leased small farms prior to 1948, it was the peasants who experienced the most wrenching change in their lives. For most in the Palestinian village population, the 1948 exodus ushered in a sudden and final exit from farming. The host Arab countries, with a growing population of their own and with limited arable land and the increasing mechanization of agriculture, were unable to absorb the Palestinian farm labor.

Notwithstanding, many younger generations of Palestinians were able to be educated, providing the largest pool of professionals and workers who, from the 1950s through the 1980s, built the infrastructures of the oil-rich Arab countries.[7]

One third of the Palestinian women's leadership was old enough to personally remember 1948, but the first generation were adults then and what they saw was recalled with unshaded emotion.

Typical is the story of Samiha Khalil, president of Ina'sh al-Usra society, which she founded in 1965. Khalil was the *graund dame* of the women's societies' movement in the West Bank and a nationalist figure who openly supported the PLO. I met Khalil at her home in Bireh one evening in the winter of 1990, just as she was concluding a meeting with representatives of neighboring women's societies. She spoke with the ease of someone who had been interviewed many times.

Khalil spoke of the time she was trapped with her family in Gaza, caught by the 1948 War. She said she stayed in Gaza for four years, unable to return to her home in the West Bank, which was less than two hours away by car. She eventually returned, but the journey was laborious and dangerous, as she traveled by small boat circuitously through the treacherous Mediterranean winter waves to Lebanon and, by land, via Syria and Jordan.

In Gaza, Khalil and her family were able to survive by staying with friends and selling Khalil's wedding jewelry for food. She knew others were not so lucky. She especially remembers the young mothers:

> Every day, young women, like flowers, would knock on the door. They would say, "Aunt would you buy this bracelet, take it for thirty—it would be expensive—take it for twenty, take it for ten. We need milk, we need bread for the children." That began a boiling in my heart.

Khalil said what she experienced in Gaza led her to ask: Why? It was less a question than an expression of her indignation and anger. She then went on to perform volunteer work and raise her young family, and, in 1965, founded Ina'sh al-Usra, which means revival of the family. Khalil began with a sewing project that relied on one machine in a garage-type setting. Now her society is housed in a large building in the outskirts of Bireh, and offers a wide array of activities including weaving, secretarial and hairdressing classes, a kindergarten, a family adoption program, and a food catering service.

Ina'sh al-Usra also houses the Museum of Palestinian Tradition, which exhibits scenes and artifacts from Palestine's rural past. Among the displays is a key to symbolize the hope for return to Palestine. It is a large iron key laid flat on a white stone shelf of the white wall, just inside the entrance to the museum. Indeed, many refugees held onto their house keys expecting to return.

Khalil and her cohorts in the first generation, and older members of the second generation, are nationalists *par excellence.* Theirs is the nationalism of cultural tradition, social community, and individual and national dignity. They are essentially centrists who, unlike the younger generations, felt no particular connection to other Third World liberation and revolutionary movements. Theirs is the nationalism of liberalism of the Arab independence movements of the 1920s and 1930s.

Their fundamental political psychology is a deep sense of "what is right," and they see their role in the national movement as preserving what was left in the social fiber after the loss of Palestine. In Khalil's words, "Our first job is to return to people their honor and pride." "We don't have a beggar nation," she said.

IV.

The younger generations learned about the 1948 events mainly from the anguished, resigned, and, sometimes reluctant, voice of a grandparent, parent, aunt, or uncle. Most, in the second generation of leaders, are about my age. I was two years old in 1948 with no memory of what occurred, but this is what I was told when I was a child. I learned that my parents had in fact made preparations to flee with small suitcases readied for the trek to the Lebanese border at Nakura, eighteen kilometers away. But the Israeli army then entered the city and we stayed.

After the occupation, the remaining Arab residents found themselves virtual prisoners and were ordered to relocate inside Old Acre—the walled part of the city—to make space for the Jewish immigrants. Old Acre also became home to hundreds of villagers from surrounding areas who found shelter in the vacant homes of refugees who had fled across the border. The new landlord was Israel's Agency of Abandoned Properties.

Among the second generation of female leaders—the twenty born between 1935 and 1948—one-third were old enough to have some memory of 1948. Fatima Bernawi is the highest ranking female in Fateh militia and is now head of the women's section of the police in the Palestinian self-rule government in the Gaza Strip and Jericho. She was barely nine when her mother fled with the children, landing temporarily in a refugee camp near Amman. (They were able to return to Jerusalem later.) Her father, who fought in the 1936 Palestinian rebellion, had remained behind in Jerusalem. Bernawi did not understand what was happening and remembers asking her mother, "Why have we immigrated?"

Bernawi belongs to a small minority of African-Palestinians (both Muslim and Christian) who lived primarily in Jerusalem. As a young woman during the mid-1950s, Bernawi experienced racial discrimination while working as a practical nurse for the Arab-American Oil Company in Saudi Arabia (ARAMCO). She said, "ARAMCO used to refuse to let me give shots because my color is Black, even though I was a Palestinian. I used to feel racial discrimination when my turn came to give shots at ARAMCO." (The Palestinian writer, Fawaz Turki, who is Caucasian, also worked for ARAMCO then, and wrote about his rage upon discovering that the toilets at ARAMCO offices were segregated into American and Arab toilets.)[8]

A decade later, Bernawi's color was used by the Israeli soldiers to arrest her for the attempted bombing of Zion Cinema in Jewish West Jerusalem. Bernawi said the bombing was in protest of showing a film that celebrated the 1967 War, but the bomb did not explode. She said, "Of course, they arrested all the young women from African origin." "As you know, my father is African," she reiterated.

The political consciousness of the second generation was woven from the mid-1950s to the mid-1960s, when Nasser of Egypt led the Arab Nationalists Movement. By then, most of the Arab countries were at least nominally independent.[9] The Palestinian elites, however, were immobilized and in disarray. All that remained was a powerless organization, the All-Palestine Committee, which survived briefly in Gaza.[10] Palestinians, like all Arabs, were in search of a new leadership that would define the Arab agenda in the post-independence era and liberate Palestine.

The second generation marched through their youth during the time of Nasser and were full of hope and dreams of change. They were compatriots of the '60s' generation in the West, in that they challenged traditional norms. But they were political allies with their disenfranchised parents, sharing with them the fundamental loss of Palestine.

What the Palestinian youth most hoped for was to realize their parents' dream of the return. The songs "Jerusalem" and "We shall return to our neighborhood" (*al-qudsu* and *sanarje'u yawman ila hayena*), by the legendary Lebanese singer Firouz, were as emotionally wrenching to the youth as they were to their parents. Also rousing were nationalist songs played to military marching tunes that beamed out of state-owned radio stations in Cairo, Damascus, and Baghdad.

At a glance, political events of the 1950s can be reduced to a list of toppled monarchies, pro-West alliances, military adventures, and a wealth of nationalist rhetoric. Anti-West sentiment grew in strides with each event: the Baghdad Pact in 1955; Egypt's nationalization of the Suez

Canal and the British, French, and Israeli invasion that followed in 1956; and the 1958 United States invasion of Lebanon.

The Middle East became a playground of the superpowers, and the Eisenhower Doctrine said the United States would fight communism there. The landing of U.S. Marines on Lebanon's shores in 1958 was its first overt application. But that year the Iraqi military toppled King Faisal, the Hashemite grandson of King Faisal of Mecca—made famous in the West by stories of T.E. Lawrence's adventures in Arabia. Also in 1958, Egypt and Syria formed the United Arab Republic.

The 1950s saw exciting Arab political movements: the Ba'ath Party (meaning *resurrection*), founded by Michel Aflaq from Syria; and the Arab Nationalists Movement, led by Palestinian George Habash. The Muslim Brotherhood, the Islamist organization started in Egypt in 1928, was also active albeit primarily underground, since it was banned by most Arab regimes that were threatened by it. However, surpassing all of these groups in popularity was Nasser, who was without peer in his charisma and popular appeal.

Nasser took center stage with the message that prosperity would come with economic development and self-sufficiency, non-alignment in the East-West competition, and Arab unity. The enemies were feudalism, "reactionaries monarchies," foreign exploitation, and Zionism. "Colonialism, revolution, and Arab nationalism" were the three most frequently used slogans in Nasser's speeches, followed by "Palestine."[11]

The liberation of Palestine was an inextricable part of Arab nationalist ethos and Arab unity was the path to achieve it. Arab nationalist rhetoric regarding Palestine echoed the 1936 words of Egyptian Muhammad Hussein Heykal: "Imperialists wish to transform Palestine into a foreign land, that is, to deprive it of its Arabism and its Islam and to detach it like a piece of flesh from the Arab body."[12]

The second generation grew up listening to Nasser deliver exciting speeches broadcast on the powerful radio frequencies of Radio Cairo and Voice of the Arabs. The speech he gave in February 1958, to announce Egypt's union with Syria, summed up the spirit of his age. He said:

> Today, my brother citizens, today is a memorable day in our history, a fateful page in our history. Today we feel that Arab nationalism indeed was realized. Today we look to the future and feel that it will be, by the help of God, full of glory and dignity. We look at the future and we look at the past and we decide from the depth of ourselves that the past will not return.[13]

It was a short-lived glory, however, unravelling with the Syrian coup in 1961 that dissolved the United Arab Republic and then the fatal blow of the 1967 Arab defeat. Nasser died three years later, just as the Palestinian Resistance was winding down its first test for survival in the Jordanian civil war of 1970–1971.

The earliest memorable events of one-fourth of the women in the second generation were student demonstrations that often erupted during the period 1955–1958. In'am Abdel Hadi (a relative of Issam) was thirteen and living in Nablus when she participated in demonstrations against the Baghdad Pact and the Eisenhower Doctrine. It was her first act of rebellion.

"I was from a conservative family that didn't accept much the idea of a female going out to a demonstration. I mean, with the young men," she explained. "Still, for sure, I had a bit of a rebellious nature for me to go out," she confessed. When I interviewed her, Abdel Hadi was living in Jordan and was a member of the secretariat of the Palestinian Lawyers Union and the Palestine National Council. She had also been married twice to Fateh leaders—one of which was assassinated in Rome.

Two women in the second generation mentioned a particular incident in 1956 or 1957 when a girl, Raja-e Abu Ammasha, was killed by the Jordanian security forces. Abu Ammasha, who was a fellow student, was shot as she lowered the British flag from the roof of the British consulate in East Jerusalem. Zahira Kamal, president of the Union of Women's Action Committees in the Occupied Territories and a leader in the Democratic Front, was one of these women.

This is how Kamal remembers the incident:

> I was nine years old in the demonstration in which Raja-e Abu Ammasha was martyred. I mean, it was the greatest shock. I mean, it affected me. . . . From that time I was active in student movements. And in secondary school I also was subjected to interrogation by Jordan. And they (the Jordanian authorities) used to have a black list and my name was in it from that time on.

Living under Arab rule in her own hometown was no guarantee of Palestinian freedom and nationalist aspirations, Kamal discovered. For Kamal, this was a very disturbing but not bizarre finding, for it seemed to have clarified her thinking about the need for Palestinians to have their own state.

While the first generation raised their families and performed volunteer work, the second generation included Arab youth who entered universities in unprecedented numbers after the mid-1950s. Nationalist regimes were fulfilling their promise of public education with new schools and universities, low-cost education, and merit-based admissions. Universities in Arab capitals, including the American University in

Beirut, made scholarships available to Palestinians. In Egypt, under Nasser, university gates were opened widely to the Gaza Strip residents who, until 1967, were under Egyptian administration.

It would have been inconceivable in the parochial towns and villages of pre-1948 Palestine to encourage, or even permit, daughters to seek education—indeed, the sons rarely had such an opportunity. Now there was an uneasy coexistence of conservative social values and a heightened interest in education in the Palestinian society.

Pass through any Palestinian city—Gaza, Khan Unis, Bethlehem, Ramallah—just before the results of the Jordanian university-qualifying examinations were announced, and you could not miss meeting parents who were anxiously awaiting the examination results. The list of those who pass appears in the newspapers and gives the names of the sons and daughters who had a chance at going to college.

The universities in Cairo, Damascus, Baghdad, and Beirut were centers of student activism. The American University of Beirut, founded in 1866 by Protestant missionaries, was a center of intellectual excitement, much like the University of California, Berkeley, in the United States. The students had their own unions, joined political parties and movements, and held informal literary and political gatherings or *nadawat*.

The cohorts of the second-generation women's leadership read Marx, Lenin, Sartre, de Beauvoir and Fanon; and they read the writings of Arab thinkers like Aflaq of the Ba'ath Party and Habash of the Arab Nationalists Movement. They also read the exciting new poetry of Mikhail Naimi, Adonis, Salah Abdel Sabbur, and Nizar al-Qabbani. Much later, in the '70s, Palestinian poets from inside Israel and the West Bank, Rashed al-Hussein, Samih al-Qassem, Fadwa Tuqan, and Mahmoud Darwish (who left Israel and was later elected to the PLO Executive Committee) were read as well.

It was not that women of the older generation did not go to the *nadawat* or read the new poetry, for these activities were common in Arab intellectual life, but that the younger generations were more fortunate to have their youth during a time of expanding educational opportunities. They found themselves in university settings where new thinking was explored on a scale never before experienced in the history of the Arab world.

In the words of In'am Abdel Hadi, who attended law school in Damascus:

> There were popular movements throughout my school years. I remember participating in all the thinking that came out of the people. I studied at the Syrian university and, at that time, we had lots of weight. The students used to be able to remove a gov-

ernment. . . . I mean the climate was very politicized, and there were political parties: the Ba'ath, the communists and the Arab Nationalists Movement. Although I didn't join any of the parties, I remained full of enthusiasm.

Also, in the early 1960s, a new secret group called *Fateh* was posed to become the nucleus of the armed resistance against Israel. Fateh was founded in the late 1950s by Arafat (nom de guerre Abu Ammar), Faruq Qaddumi (Abu Lutuf), Khalil al-Wazir (Abu Jihad), and Salah Khalaf (Abu Iyad), men who began their political careers as university students in Cairo. Fateh founders were teachers, businessmen, and engineers, working in Syria, Libya, Gaza, and the Gulf region.

Secretly, they recruited, led commando raids, raised funds, and distributed underground messages that called for the armed struggle to liberate Palestine. In a few years, Fateh and other Palestinian factions or *fasa'il* would resort to armed struggle and in doing so would change politics in the Palestinian society, replacing the *zu'ama* (traditional leaders, mainly mayors and village chiefs) with *fida'iyyin* (those who were willing to sacrifice their life for their cause).

Among the first supporters were Um Lutuf and Um Jihad, second-generation women who were the young wives of Fateh pioneers. (Not all the wives took on political roles; for example, the wife of Abu Iyad remained inactive.) Um Lutuf has been in Fateh since the late 1950s, when she married Abu Lutuf, who became head of its cadre organization. Um Lutuf remembers how her husband sat her down, just before their wedding, to talk about what she was getting into. She said:

He said, "Will you carry the responsibility. I tell you there are three things that can burn a revolutionary: gambling, money and women." He told me, "Gambling and money I can take care of, but will you be able to make the journey with me?"[14]

Um Lutuf understood what her marriage to a revolutionary entailed and was enthusiastic to join her husband. In those early years, she helped him by doing secretarial work for his essays in Fateh's underground leaflets. She also tried to organize women, first in Cairo, while working with the Palestinian Women's League (the women's society led by Abu Ghazaleh) and, later, in Kuwait and Syria, where her family also lived.

Outside the few who were among Fateh's pioneers or had worked in the women's societies' movement, the majority of the women's leadership became focused on the Palestinian cause in the aftermath of the 1967 War and the Arab defeat. In fact, for the second and third generations of leadership, the 1967 War was the single most politicizing event of their lives.

V.

In the 1967 War, Israel occupied the West Bank and Gaza Strip (also the Egyptian Sinai Desert and the Syria Golan Heights). It was the first Arab-Israeli conflict personally experienced by all three generations. If the Israeli occupation of the West Bank and Gaza Strip was *déjà vu* for the first generation, reviving dormant pain from the 1948 catastrophe, for the second and third generations, it was a confirmation of long-held fears—that Israel could reach them even in the mighty Arab capitals. This deep sense of vulnerability was somewhat new in modern Arab political pathos and its impact on the thinking of members of the women's leadership can be heard in several of their accounts.

"This was the first time I saw my father look defeated," said third-generation Salwa Mustafa, a PLO official who is Tunisian by birth and Palestinian by marriage. Mustafa has worked for years in a high level husband-wife team, most recently in Tunis for Abu Mazen, head of the PLO's National Relations Department.

Women's Union secretariat member Khadijeh Abu Ali was living in Amman and in her last year of college when she decided to join the Palestinian Resistance in 1968, giving up pursuing a graduate degree in educational psychology. (In 1976, Abu Ali published the first book ever on the participation of women in the Palestinian movement.)[15] She said:

> When I grew up, I began to have strong awareness that the presence of Israel in the region is doing great oppression and injustice to the Palestinian and Arab individual and that it is an obstacle to our progress as a society. It was a threat to me especially after 1967 happened and I was still at university. I felt what is the use of my education if, at any moment, someone will come sweep the country and occupy it. And I might die. The only thing, I felt, had meaning at that time was to struggle until one gets these people out, until one liberates this region and one can breath, build one's country and develop one's abilities as a human. That is how it started.

Lawyer's Union secretariat member In'am Abdel Hadi grew up comfortably in Nablus and, like most in the Palestinian upper-middle class, was quite shielded from the hardships that resulted from the Palestinian dismemberment, until she learned about the eruption of the 1967 War while she was living in Damascus and attending law school. It was during her journey back to Nablus, West Bank, to be with her family, that the refugee experience was brought home.

Abdel Hadi said she was forced to stay overnight in a refugee camp set up by the Red Cross on the Jordanian side of the border. She still remembers what she ate at night, "a tomato, bread and salt," distributed by the International Red Cross. "It was very sad and I felt myself a refugee," she said. Soon she returned to Amman where she took her law examinations, worked for a while in television (but later practiced law) and, in 1969, joined Fateh.

Ashrawi, the former peace negotiator who lives in the West Bank, said she was politically awakened while studying at the American University in Beirut:

> I was sixteen when I went to the university. It was my first encounter with real poverty—when I went to the camps in Lebanon—my first encounter with real misery. We were very sheltered, very protected before the (Israeli) occupation. Nineteen-sixty-seven is the landmark when I felt I had to do something and that each individual makes a difference.

PLO Ambassador Shahid, who grew up in Beirut, was also attending the American University. She said:

> After the defeat of 1967, in 1968, I entered university and, in the first year of university, Beirut airport was bombarded by the Israeli military. The second day university students began to organize military training so that we can defend ourselves. "How is it that the Israeli air force could come to the center of Beirut City?" I entered politics from that period.

The 1967 War had a powerful impact on Rabiha Diyab who is head of the Social Work Committees in the Occupied Territories and is Fateh's top female cadre in the West Bank. She spent her adult years in and out of Israeli prison—once in 1990, shortly after our first meeting. Diyab was an adolescent during the 1967 War. She remembered:

> Maybe I was twelve years of age during the 1967 War. There was the Israeli occupation of the remaining part of Palestine—contrary to what we expected. We used to learn in school about the Algerian Jamilah Buhrayd and in poetry that told of her role in the struggle for her country against France. I used to think, as was said, the Arabs would liberate Palestine after one or two years. I was the kind who loved to say: my God, I hope that Palestine would not be liberated until I finish secondary school, finish my education so that I can participate in the struggle.

In Palestinian history, the 1967 War was the event that unleashed Palestinian and Arab rage, bringing thousands of young people knocking on the gates of Fateh and other rapidly formed Palestinian militias.

Palestinian youth thought they could finally have their day with Israel. There were secret cells and militia camps; mass organizations like the students' and women's unions; and a growing revolutionary media of small secretly distributed leaflets and pamphlets that espoused the ideas of the Palestinian Revolution.

Two factions took center stage and remained there to represent the ideological and organizational poles of the Palestinian National Movement. The Arafat-led Fateh supported a Palestinian nationalist agenda, saying the slogan, "Arab unity for the liberation of Palestine" died in the 1967 War. These words, which during Nasser's time seemed indelible, were replaced with "The liberation of Palestine is the road to Arab unity." Fateh soon flourished and its organization moved from its clandestine existence to become a catchall, loosely organized party whose ranks gathered Marxist-Leninists, Ba'athists, Muslim Brothers—but mainly patriots uncomfortable with all ideological labels.

The Popular Front for the Liberation of Palestine was essentially the Palestine branch of the Arab Nationalists Movement, led by George Habash. After the 1967 defeat, the Popular Front adopted an armed struggle strategy and in 1968 also embraced Marxism-Leninism, to "give the Palestinian Revolution its class content," it said. However, the group soon learned that atheism and class struggle held little appeal among the conservative Palestinian mainstream whose most urgent battle was for the homeland.

The Popular Front remained small, appealing mainly to members of the urban, better-educated classes, but its influence on the Palestinian movement went beyond its size. The Front represented a long-active current in the Palestinian left, and its plane hijackings in the late 1960s and early 1970s brought it further national recognition. But in the long term, the Front was able to survive and keep its role of "loyal opposition" by maintaining a secretive, tightly organized, and well-trained cadre organization.

The Palestinian factions were the organizational home of second- and third-generation leaders. These women were contemporaries of the Arab nationalist revival, but had become impatient with the resignation of their parents' generation, and with the old rhetoric of the protracted Arab war to liberate Palestine. They looked for role models in Mao Tse-tung and other heroes of Third World revolutionary movements, and thought armed struggle and popular mobilization were the way to liberate Palestine.[16] They were fairly young, mostly in their teens and 20s. Not yet invested in marriage and raising children—some having postponed that to attend college—they were receptive to the risky political lives upon which they would embark. And the Palestinian factions provided the framework and the opportunities.

The major upheavals—the 1948 War, the turbulent 1950s and 1960s, the 1967 War—were events commonly experienced by the bulk of the Palestinian people (and the Arab world in general). In themselves, these events shed some light on why certain individuals made a lifelong commitment to the Palestinian cause. How is it that certain women were able to break out of long-honored norms of behavior for the Arab female that prescribed fundamentally private and social roles—not political ones? In the case of the Palestinian women's leadership, the answer lies in an extraordinary social and familial background.

VI.

At a glance, these women appear inconspicuous. Like most in the urban Arab middle class, their attire is modest and modern (not the traditional long dress commonly worn by older women in the villages and refugee camps)—none wore the Muslim veil. But their background was anything but ordinary.

Two-thirds were born into families that have had some involvement in politics. There were government officials, community activists, labor union organizers, and rebels. Ideologically, there were Arab nationalists, socialists and communists—but not Islamists, confirming the secular nature of the Palestinian movement.

These political relations are an important part of the women's childhood memories and are noted with pride: "My father, before me, was a political person, I mean, a Palestinian fighter." "Mother struggled since her student days." "My father was deported to Syria during the time of the Hussein (of Mecca) Revolt." "Mother was a revolutionary against the French Mandate." "Father was the provincial governor of Horan (in Syria)." "Father was in the Jordanian parliament." "Father was a socialist and a feminist." And, "Father used to collect funds to distribute to Palestinian students in Alexandria."

In sharp contrast, all nine women from the Popular and Democratic fronts said they (and one or two siblings) were the first politicos in their families, a phenomenon I am unable to explain fully. These women were from the second and third generations but that does not explain their distinction since Fateh's women are also primarily from these generations. The ability for the fronts' women to enter politics on their own certainly reflects the receptivity and encouragement of the leftist factions. At the same time, the explanation lies in part in the family background of the women of Fateh, which has always attracted nationalist families. (And I would also add that Fateh has benefitted from support of prominent nationalist families such as the Husaynis of Jerusalem, the Abdel Hadis of Nablus, and the Shawwas of Gaza, who were pro-Jordanian as well.)

On the whole, as are most older Palestinians, their parents were relatively uneducated and several of the mothers were illiterate. At the same time, a significant segment was exceptionally well-educated; one-quarter of the fathers—but only two of the mothers—were college graduates.[17] The women themselves are a highly educated group regardless of factional affiliation. All but one completed her secondary education; over two-thirds graduated from college, including two from law school; and one-quarter earned graduate degrees (in a variety of fields, including sociology, psychology, literature, mathematics, and physics).

Did their educational and political background pave the way for these women to become involved in the liberation struggle? Probably so. But these facilitators did not send them far outside the boundaries of the Arab, indeed universal, social norm of the traditional gender roles. The Arab term women often used in their interviews was *khosusiat al-mar'a*, roughly meaning, "the special situation of women." Khosusiat al-mar'a refers to the collection of private and social obligations and restrictions on a female's mobility, and has the end result of eliminating or, at least, inhibiting the opportunity to pursue an active public life. (This was not a problem for those leading the charitable societies, because their contributions were considered respectable social service—proper roles for women in the more prosperous families.)

In Arab society, the roles of daughter, wife, and mother are inextricably bound to the norm of honor, which is a precondition of female marriageability. The two elements of honor are the female's sexual reputation or *al-'ird* and the family's own standing in the community or *karamah*.[18] The prime guardians of honor are the men in the family—the father and, in his absence, the older son, and the husband after marriage. When none of these males exist and there are no males from the extended family to take charge, the "provider and protector" responsibilities then fall on the mother and the older daughter. In practice, that means that the young female must secure the consent of her guardian if she wants to attend college, seek employment, or become involved in organizations. Political involvement meant closer interaction with unrelated males—and that could cause "people to talk." The women who joined the militia in the late 1960s were particularly susceptible to accusations of "loose behavior."[19]

The crux of the women's honor question is that a reputation of "loose behavior" dishonors the family by saying it somehow failed at protecting its daughters. This norm still lingers in Palestinian society—even among the educated, although much less potently, and it is felt by both Muslims and Christians (who comprise around 5 percent of Palestinians and five of the thirty-four women leaders).

The norm of honor is especially strong in the smaller towns and villages and in large and closely knit families, where parents must consider the reputation of the wider network of the extended family. It is much easier if the woman lives outside the ancestral area and in urban areas, which was the case of most of the women leaders. In these more open social environments, keeping up appearances no longer precludes socializing with males, and certainly not at the universities that are coeducational.

In the end, the matter of reputation was settled within the bounds of the home, and travel outside the hometown proved to be the main test. Eisheh Odeh won her battle early when she overcame her mother's resistance to continuing her education beyond the elementary level, which meant a journey to the nearby town. The decision was the mother's because the father was dead and the older brother was living in Brazil. Odeh's mother feared, "What will people say," especially since no other girl had ever done so in the village—not even the daughter of the village *mukhtar* or chief, the mother had said.

It took a hunger strike by young Odeh to bend her mother's will and she became the first girl in her village to finish her secondary education. Odeh had hoped to go on to university but instead joined the resistance, becoming one of its first female guerrillas. However, in her middle age, Odeh resumed her university education at Jordan's Yarmuk University.

In the two cases where the consent of the mother was needed and received, the decision was supported by the oldest brother, which helped ease the mother's apprehension. But in all the cases, parental (or husband's) consent was all that was needed. With one or two exceptions, community "talk" never materialized and moreover the women's commitment to the national movement appeared to have brought them respect in their communities.

The women's participation in the Palestinian National Movement was at first secret, delaying the dreaded confrontation with parents. When confrontations with parents—mainly fathers—ensued, the discussions revealed a complexity that went deeper than, "What will people say?" Here is a sample.

In the late 1960s, Jehan Helou was living in Beirut, a large metropolis long known for its social openness. She was already one of Fateh's top female cadres and soon would become a leader in the Women's Union. This is how she summarized the argument with her father when she requested his permission to travel outside the country. She said:

Once my father didn't want me to travel abroad. I was going with a delegation in 1969. I had to argue and argue and he was apparently afraid for me. And then I said, "I don't have any brothers. I feel very bad I was born a girl." And my father—he was rather democratic—said, "Why?" He was hurt. And I said—maybe this was tactical,"—If I was a boy I would just say I am going because I have graduated from the university." Imagine that I still had to. . . . And if I was a boy that is all he would have told his father. And he said, "No." And he laughed. And I laughed. And that was it, and I travelled. You see, I think every one of us had to struggle on two fronts.

Some of the parents expressed concern about securing a comfortable social life for their daughters. This was noted by Um Lutuf, Eileen Kuttab and Laila Shahid—all from highly educated, urban families. When Um Lutuf decided to marry Fateh leader Abu Lutuf (sometime in the late 1950s), her father chided her for settling for the modest standard of living that joining the resistance would incur.

In the early '70s, Kuttab was a young student at the American University in Beirut and was also very active politically in the student group of the Popular Front (later she became a leader in the Union of Palestinian Women's Committees in the West Bank). She said she was expelled from the University for her political activism, and that her expulsion, of course, got back to her parents. She summed up her parents' response this way:

My family's reaction was not bad, but they were afraid like all families who fear for their children's arrest, etc. They used to say, serving the homeland is good, but you must know how to serve it, you must study and learn good knowledge.

Shahid was living with her family in Beirut in 1970 and was already a member of Fateh. She said:

I remember that my father and mother were surprised because they first knew the day I came to tell them that I want to go to Amman in 1970 to attend the congress of the (Palestinian) student union. They were surprised to discover that I have clear interest in politics. Since childhood I had wanted to study medicine. My father said, "If you are going to work in politics, you are not going to make it in medicine because medicine is a very serious matter."

But her mother was very pleased because, Shahid said, "In a way, what her generation couldn't do my generation is doing."

Once married (all but six eventually were), the role of family protector was transferred to the husband, and his support became crucial.

Ashrawi's public speaking for the Intifada and the peace process received the full support of her husband:

> I am very fortunate because my husband is quite liberated. He ends up doing most of the work at home. . . . And he says he feels that I can do more in politics and in my work than he can, and he would prefer to spend more time at home with the girls, with my daughters, and he does.

Um Nasser, member of the Women's Union secretariat and former head of the PLO chairman's office, was in her early 30s and childless when, in 1967, she decided to join Fateh. In the traditional Arab custom, she asked her husband's permission. Their discussion was serious and frank about what it meant to make a commitment to Fateh. She told the story with a hint of relaxed amusement in her voice.

Um Nasser said she told her husband, "Think about it, wait till morning. Don't hurry because you will pay a price for my commitment oath. I shall belong to Fateh forever; my hair even will no longer be mine." "There is no need to think about it," her husband replied, "here is the key to my house. If you have all this conviction and ambition and you are able to give, why not?"

Their marriage, however, ended in divorce, but that was after Um Nasser moved with the Palestinian Resistance out of Jordan in 1971. Going with the Resistance to Lebanon also resulted in Mai Sayigh's divorce, and she also lost custody of her young children. For most in the women's leadership, political involvement in the liberation struggle meant compromise regarding the issue of having children.

In an Arab society, where the standard is to raise several children, the women's leadership averaged only two children each. Helou and her husband decided not to have children, which then subjected them to unbearable social pressure. "Many of our friends took the same decision, but they couldn't go on with the decision," she said. "We thought we wanted to be full-timers, both of us. And we were not settled," she explained.

How the women with children squared their political activities with raising children varied. Some, like Ashrawi and Abdel Hadi, had a great deal of help from family members. Most were not so fortunate. Member of the Women's Union secretariat, Abu Ali, said:

> I gave birth to two children in very difficult circumstances because of the cause in our life, the Palestinian people. There were periods in which we had to immigrate from one place to the other. In certain periods there were wars. It wasn't easy to give birth and build a stable family.

Another member of the Women's Union, Um Sabri, lost her Fateh-commander husband during the fighting in the Jordanian civil war when she was just a young bride. Thus she had to raise her two infants alone. "My giving was always on the expense of the children," she said, adding, "I used to try to balance between my children and my work as much as possible even at cost to my health and personal matters."

Several met their husbands through the movement. Nine of these men were from the PLO leadership and, altogether, five have died (three violently), which earned the widows the revered title "wife of martyr." To have a comrade husband, however, did not always guarantee that the husbands shared the responsibilities at home.

Nihaya Muhammad was member of the Women's Union secretariat since the early years in Lebanon and is in the leadership of the Democratic Front. She said having a husband who works in the same field helped a lot because he understood her political responsibilities. Maha Nassar was head of the Union of Palestinian Women's Committees in the Occupied Territories while raising her young family. She said it was difficult even when her husband, also a comrade, helped.

"Most of the housework falls on me, from the children to the cooking and cleaning," Nassar said. "The female fighter in our society pays the price twice," she concluded, "once because she is a woman and another because she is a fighter."

And fighters they were, though only a few ever fit the stereotypical image of the Palestinian freedom fighter—the kaleshnikov-toting fatigues and kaffiyeh-dressed militant. (The kaffiyeh is the checkered headdress and kerchief worn by traditional Arab men and was an insignia of PLO chairman Arafat.) The preponderant element in their long political careers was working in popular mobilization, and they did it in the best tradition of the partisan who displays an unmistakable commitment to the cause, tempered with a deep sense of personal autonomy—and sometimes independence of thought. Most found their contributions bounded inside the women's sphere of activity they called the "women's frameworks."[20] Only four: Laila Khaled, Fatima Bernawi, Eisheh Odeh, and Rasmiyeh Odeh became active first as guerrillas. All were from the second generation who enrolled with the first waves of recruits to the Palestinian National Movement. Their fighting careers, however, were brief.

VIII.

Laila Khaled spent much of her political life working in Lebanon and Syria in the women's framework of the Popular Front. She was the Front's top woman, representing it in the Women's Union secretariat during the

'70s and after as head of its women's organization, founded in 1980. Khaled began her involvement in the Popular Front as a guerrilla and is best known for her plane hijackings (a TWA in 1969 and an El Al in 1970). In the early '70s, however, she abandoned her fighting role when, she said, she became easily recognizable.[21] (In her middle years, Khaled's hijackings came back to haunt her in the concerned voice of her seven-year-old son who one day asked: "Mother, do you steal planes?")

The other three guerrillas—Fateh's Fatima Bernawi, Democratic Front's Eisheh Odeh, and Popular Front's Rasmiyeh Odeh (who is apparently unrelated to Eisheh)—were living in the West Bank in 1967 when the armed resistance movement erupted. The three women soon became part of the first recruits but all were captured by the Israelis within a year or two.

Each of the three was sentenced to life imprisonment and each completed ten years of her sentence before being released—Bernawi for health reasons and the two Odehs in prisoner exchanges. Prison, however, was a place where the women could sharpen their political skills and, in fact, each exhibited a talent for leadership that brought praise from their prison comrades, helping to elevate them inside their respective factions. This was especially true of Eisheh Odeh, who went on to become a member of the Democratic Front's Political Bureau.

I first interviewed Odeh in September 1991 in Amman, where she worked in the PLO's social services agency, Families of the Martyrs foundation; she also was attending classes at Yarmuk University. On several occasions, during my previous visit in 1990, female comrades in the Democratic Front in the Occupied Territories spoke admiringly of her and said I must interview her—something I had already planned to do.

My interest in Odeh was enhanced when I listened to the Palestinian poet Fadwa Tuqan give a reading of a poem dedicated to Odeh at East Jerusalem's al-Hakawati theater. The poem, "A small song to despair," was inspired by a letter Odeh had sent to the poet from the Central Prison in Nablus where she was incarcerated; and it was meant to be a note of hope.[22] In prison, Odeh was called the "flower of autumn" because of her ability to lift morale.

Rawda al-Basiir, a fellow former prisoner, gave an example from her own experience when she first met Odeh. Al-Basiir, a leader in the Union of Women's Action Committees in Nablus, related the story as we walked through the streets of her town, where I visited some of the projects of the women's committees. Al-Basiir was fifteen when she first entered prison, and Odeh was there to receive her:

> Here she was: someone who had been tortured and raped by the Israelis and was serving a life sentence. I imagined her looking

aged with stringy white hair—and here I was exhausted and my arm in a sling. Instead, Eisheh looked young, her hair nice, and she said to me, "I smell Tireh in you."

Odeh had extended warm greetings to the teenager by way of recognizing her village. And other political prisoners will relate how they formed close communities in prison, which provided political and emotional support and mentorship. It was a connectedness that lasted beyond time in prison and is remembered fondly.

Altogether, about one-third of the thirty-four leaders experienced Israeli interrogation and imprisonment (and two were sexually tortured). Issam Abdel Hadi was forced to see her fifteen-year-old daughter beaten in front of her to get a confession (more on that in the next chapter). To varying degrees, all the women in the leadership had a brush with violence, which is not unexpected given the nature of their involvement. The female freedom fighters who served long sentences in Israeli prison, however, were an elite group who became heroic figures from the period of the late 1960s through the 1970s—the armed struggle stage of the Palestinian movement.

Every one of these women paid a high personal price that further deepened her political commitment. Indeed, each of their personal struggles and tragedies helped propel them to leadership roles. For about one-third of the women, certainly those from the more traditional Fateh, being a wife or a sister of a leading man were crucial facilitators for their recruitment to the women's leadership. For all, lasting loyalty to their factions and political connections were necessary for political survival. But these facts must not reduce the value of the women's individual sacrifices and perseverance. In the end, both an unusual social, political background, and unmistakable resilience best explains their attainment of leadership. In their own words, however, they simply called their lifelong careers "the work" or *al-'amal* and, for the first generation, it began in the mid-1960s on the eve of the Palestinian National Movement.

Chapter 2

AMMAN
Early Years of the Revolutionary Struggle

I.

The Palestinian National Movement began during the period 1967–1971 in the aftermath of the 1967 War in which Israel defeated its Arab neighbors and occupied parts of Egypt, Syria and the Palestinian West Bank and Gaza Strip. These were the Palestinian territories that, following the armistice agreements between Israel and its Arab neighbors in the 1948 War, came under the control of Jordan and Egypt respectively until June 1967. During its initial years, the liberation movement gathered steam from Palestinians throughout their diaspora but was centered in Jordan. The country bordered the newly occupied Palestinian territories and had a huge Palestinian population of its own, including thousands in the refugee camps in and around Amman. Therefore, it was a natural ground for the leadership of various Palestinian armed factions to set up offices and guerrilla camps.

The Jordanian period was brief but pivotal in Palestinian history in that it witnessed rise of the Palestinian armed struggle movement to regain Palestine. The highlight of this period was the guerrilla raids on Israel and the famous 1968 battle of Karameh, where Palestinian fighters rebuffed the Israeli regulars who crossed to Jordan to attack the guerrillas operating out of that border village. But the most devastating development of that period was the civil war between the Jordanian military and the Palestinian guerrillas, who had found a receptive environment in Jordan's refugee camps. The Jordanian-Palestinian honeymoon proved to be very brief, lasting less than two years. Afterwards, the Jordanian government moved to drive out the Palestinian guerrillas from its territory, concluding that the Palestinian resistance, especially its more radical elements, posed a serious threat to the regime and to keeping a semblance of a peaceful border with its strong neighbor Israel. The Jordanian civil war consisted of a few battles and skirmishes during the period 1970–1971. It ended when the Palestinians agreed to halt all military and political activity in Jordan. Later, the guerrillas and institutions of the Palestinian movement moved to Lebanon, where they remained until driven out by Israel in 1982.

The Jordanian period was a transitional stage during which the leadership of Palestinians was taken over by the factions of the armed resistance. Factional leadership replaced control by the Arab countries and the internal power of traditional Palestinian notable families, mayors, and village chiefs. This was the context of the transformation of the women's leadership itself, which now encompassed women from the factions as well as women from the charitable societies and, at the end of the Jordanian period, the women's leadership was effectively taken over by the factions, mainly Fateh.

General secretary of the Palestinian Women's Union Abu Khadra is one of Fateh's female pioneers and is among the rare few from the first generation who made the transition from the women's societies to the armed struggle movement. Abu Khadra and Um Lutuf symbolize women who initially worked with charitable societies but who in fact were already committed to Fateh's strategy of armed struggle, which began clandestinely in the late 1950s. In that sense, Abu Khadra also represents continuity and legitimacy in the Palestinian women's leadership. In her words:

> It is not because we have been here from the beginning that we are better than other women. But we, of course, have a long stamina. Because of good fortune, we were from the pioneers and have persisted. So we represent legitimacy in some form or other to reach the homeland, to reach the state. After that the nation will choose who it wants.

The first step in formalizing the engagement of the women's leadership in nationalist politics occurred prior to the rise of the Palestinian resistance when, in 1964, the PLO was established in Cairo by Jamal Abdel Nasser, leader of Egypt, under the auspices of the Arab League of States. The convening of the first session of the PLO's representative body, the Palestinian National Council, set the stage for a more enhanced and direct involvement by women.

Until 1967, the most prominent female Palestinian figures were leaders of women's charitable societies operating in the East Jerusalem-Beirut-Cairo Arab urban nexus. Best known and active longest, even before the

1948 Catastrophe, were the aging Wadi'a al-Khartabil who resided in Beirut after fleeing in 1948, Zuleikha al-Shihabi in Jerusalem, and a younger Issam Abdel Hadi in Nablus. New additions to the women's societies' leadership were Yusra Barbari in Gaza, Samiha Khalil in Bireh, and Samira Abu Ghazaleh in Cairo. Abu Ghazaleh's Palestinian Women's League was founded in 1963 and Barbari's Palestine Women's Union and Khalil's Ina'sh al-Usra in 1965. All these women were well-known nationalists, but in the absence of a Palestinian body politic after 1948, their activities were solely and necessarily social.

All that changed in the mid-1960s. First, the General Union of Palestinian Women was formed in 1965 as a mobilizational organization affiliated with the PLO and committed to the Palestinian struggle. Second, the rise of the Palestinian National Movement in the aftermath of the 1967 War brought about a transfer of women's leadership from the societies to the resistance.

In 1965, the Women's Union secretariat was dominated by figures from the societies led by Abdel Hadi. It was headquartered in Jerusalem. From the period 1966–1974, the union was headquartered in Cairo due to a ban on its activities imposed by Jordan. Consequently, Abdel Hadi, who lived in Nablus (until 1969) under the new Israeli occupation, was unable to direct the affairs of her union. Instead, until the union's Second Congress in Beirut in 1974, the Cairo branch—which was actually Abu Ghazaleh's Palestinian Women's League—was officially in charge.

In reality, by 1969, women from the first generation and older women from the second generation who belonged to Fateh—Salwa Abu Khadra, Um Nasser, Um Lutuf, and Mai Sayigh—had taken charge of the union's leadership. Sayigh was the operational head as the union's deputy chief (later renamed general secretary), a post always held by women from Fateh, which is the dominant faction. Active at the hubs of the Palestinian National Movement in Amman and Damascus, they presided over the first recruitment drive of the union, bringing in new blood from students and recent university graduates and the refugee camps in Jordan and Syria.

In the late 1960s, Fateh was an enthusiastic young movement, but one that was reluctant to shake up the conservative social values of the Palestinian society. Its centrist orientation appealed to the socially conservative population of the refugee camps as well as the Palestinian middle class. The leading place of women of Fateh in the Women's Union, however, was as much a function of their cautious approach to activism, which appealed to the predominantly conservative population, as to their familial and friendship connections to Fateh leaders. This was especially true in the case of Um Nasser and Mai Sayigh, friends of Arafat. Sayigh was from Gaza, hometown of Arafat and several other Fateh leaders. It is "a kind of tribalism" that prevailed early on, said one observer. Salwa Abu Khadra's leadership, however, must be fully attributed to the fact that she was among the very first to commit to Fateh. In the end, these women led in the Union because their faction, Fateh, dominated the PLO.

A handful of the thirty-four women—those in the first generation and older ones in the second—played key roles in these developments during the Jordan period. More important, the changing of the guard from the charitable societies to the Armed Resistance was accompanied by an unprecedented leap of women into the nationalist arena; indeed, their contributions were among the cornerstones of the Palestinian National Movement. Now, over two decades later, memories have begun to fade about all that occurred, and what follows is a distillation of the original ideas, discussions, and projects.

II.

The year 1964 was a particularly important turning point in the Palestinian struggle for self-determination and statehood. The first session of the Palestine National Council was convened in East Jerusalem, and it was the largest gathering of Palestinian politicians since the 1948 Catastrophe. The National Council had come into existence as a representative and policymaking body of the PLO, propelled into existence by Nasser. The PLO itself was still mainly a shell consisting of a skeletal operation out of an office in Cairo.[1] In 1968, the PLO was taken over by the resistance forces who transformed it from a symbol of Arab determination and nationalism to the embodiment of Palestinian national aspirations.

What could not have escaped many at the first session of the National Council was that Palestinian women had come to the meeting in force (45 present and 21 sitting as delegates, out of a total of 422.) About half of these women represented the charitable societies in the West Bank; the remainder represented Palestinian geographic regions and communities. The council makeup had followed the old tradition of having the "notables" speak for the people; these were mayors and village chiefs, representatives of prosperous families, Muslim and Christian patriarchs, and leaders of the charitable societies.

In the late 1960s, when the militia organizations took control of the PLO, women in the National Council practically disappeared, reflecting the fact that their numbers among the fighters were quite small. In the late 1970s, however, the factions' non-fighting organizations—the popular unions and professional and worker syndicates—grew in strength in terms of their contributions to the movement and, consequently, in the

National Council. This was reflected in the increase of women delegates—most of whom were from the Women' Union list. Their representation finally leveled at 9 percent in the mid-1980s.

The Jerusalem meeting was held three years before the Palestinian National Movement exploded, following the 1967 War, and four years before the Armed Resistance factions took control of the PLO. Abdel Hadi was a member of the National Council (and would continue to be for the rest of her political life), as were Samiha Khalil, Zuleikha al-Shihabi and Wadi'a al-Khartabil. Al-Shihabi, along with Milia al-Sakakini, was founder of the Arab Palestinian Women's Union, the longest running women's charitable society, active in Jerusalem since the 1930s. Both Abdel Hadi and al-Shihabi were in the preparatory committee of the National Council.

In addition to their participation in the preparations for the 1964 session, Abdel Hadi and her colleagues also got passed a resolution that supported "the participation of the Palestinian Arab woman in all aspects of organizational work in the struggle and the equality with the man in all rights and duties in order to liberate Palestine."[2] It was, of course, a symbolic achievement at best because, in reality, the National Council had no power to implement its will, since the bulk of the Palestinian people lived under the jurisdiction of the Arab and Israeli states. And these states prohibited, or at best restrained, political expression among their Palestinian populations. But the National Council resolution was important symbolically because it established the goal of gender equality in Palestinian society—a principle the Palestinian National Movement continued to espouse.

Another development during the period 1964–1965 was the formation of the General Union of Palestinian Women. It came about when the head of the PLO Department of Popular Organizations invited representatives from the women's societies from the West Bank and Gaza Strip to form a national organization for women, for the purpose of mobilizing them for the national struggle. (At that time, only one Palestinian union existed—the General Union of Palestine Students—but other unions and syndicates were formed later.) The idea of forming the Women's Union was not a novel one, for societies' leader, al-Khartabil, had made that same proposal at a general meeting of the charitable societies in 1963. It was only in the next two years that the idea gained momentum, with the convening of the National Council.

The preparatory congress for the Women's Union met in Jerusalem during the week of July 15–21, 1965, and consisted of 139 participants—almost all from the societies. Most of the women from the first generation were there, and societies' leader Al-Shihabi presided over the meeting.

Also attending was Fateh insider, twenty-three-year-old Um Jihad (who said she was the youngest there). Um Jihad was representing Fateh, which had just emerged out of secrecy in January of that year by announcing its purpose to wage armed struggle against Israel. The formation of the Women's Union in 1965 was an important moment in the history of the Palestinian women's leadership because it gave them an openly political framework for involvement in nationalist politics.

The key question settled in 1965 was this: Should the charitable societies be entangled with politics—which meant organized participation in the liberation struggle? This was a new debate for the Palestinian women who had participated in their independence struggle only sporadically, having been left out of political organizations by the customs of gender segregation and male exclusive control of public affairs, and by not having political outlets of their own.

Palestinian women participated in the national struggle mostly by raising funds, petitioning, demonstrating and staging sit-ins to protest the British occupation. For example, in the Palestinian Rebellion of 1936, women gave pieces of their jewelry to buy ammunition and also collected clothing for the Palestinian fighters. It was also reported that a few women in the villages had carried guns and fought.[3] But charitable work was the backbone of women's participation; it was steady, solid, and enduring, but always seen as essentially social in character thus relegated to the background of public political consciousness.

Al-Shihabi thought the charitable societies should keep their social character because it could be dangerous to be openly political. If they affiliated officially with the PLO, they could become subject to harassment, or worse, banning. She asked, who then would take care of the urgent needs of the community? Abdel Hadi understood al-Shihabi's position, but she herself opted for the union—and was elected its president. Most in the women's societies' leadership, however, were reluctant to be more openly political and so remained outside the union.

The first few years of the Women's Union were uneventful, especially in terms of mobilizational work. One year after its establishment in Jerusalem, the Union was banned by the Jordanian authorities (who controlled the West Bank during the period 1948–1967), and after Israel took over in 1967 the ban became permanent. The reason for the Jordanian ban was that the union had engaged in unauthorized sit-ins and demonstrations to protest the Israeli attack on Samu', a village located in the hills near Bethlehem on the Jordanian side of the 1967 Jordanian-Israeli border. Abdel Hadi and her colleagues had made the government angry when they protested Jordanian reluctance to confront Israel about the killing of the Palestinian villagers. The ban, coming so soon after the founding of the union, left it partially paralyzed until the time it was infused by the new energy of the women from the Armed Resistance.

In 1969, Abdel Hadi and al-Shihabi were deported to Jordan after being accused by Israel of participating in resisting the occupation. The last straw as far as the Israel authorities were concerned was the staging by the women's charitable societies of a sit-in and hunger strike, held at the gates of Jerusalem's Church of the Holy Sepulchre. The event was staged to protest the killing of three women and the wounding of thirteen others by Israeli soldiers outside Gaza prison. The women who were attacked were local women from Rafah and Khan Yunis in the Gaza Strip; they had gone to the prison to request entry to visit their male relatives after hearing that they were being tortured inside. Refused entry to the prison, they then tried to storm it, which is when they were shot.[4]

Some months after their deportation, al-Shihabi was able to return to Jerusalem after arguing successfully with the Israeli authorities that her organization was only charitable in nature. The Women's Union president could make no such case and had to remain in Amman in exile until mid-1993.[5]

Before being deported, Abdel Hadi was kept for a few months in prison, where she was interrogated. This experience left a lasting imprint on her because the Israeli interrogators tortured her daughter in front of her to force her to confess. It was the hardest thing she's ever had to endure, she said. She also remembers what her interrogator said, "You were behind the Palestinian woman's confusion." As she spoke of the event, during our 1990 interview in Amman, her indignation resurfaced. She said, "They called it confusion. They didn't acknowledge that it is a kind of resistance."

The year 1969 marked the complete passage of Abdel Hadi from the safety of charitable work to the open advocacy of armed resistance. From that time on, she remained an active member of the National Council by virtue of her role as the Women's Union president. And, for many years, she was the only woman in the Central Council—the smaller leadership body of the National Council that makes decisions when the full body is not in session.

If Abdel Hadi had been born in the United States, or any other democracy, she would have been the kind of community leader who is a reliable partisan during election campaigns, one capable of raising large sums of money and getting out the vote. But in the context of a national liberation movement, she had settled for a nonpartisan role, typical of her charitable societies background. When all is said, however, Abdel Hadi's forte is her resilience and single-mindedness, the characteristics that best portray the first generation of political Palestinians—the men and women who have been involved in the cause as far back as the 1948 events.

III.

The 1967 War between Israel and its Arab neighbors and the Arab defeat that followed gave birth to new phrases in the Palestinian political culture, such as "the armed struggle," "the resistance," "the revolution," and others that signified the re-birth of Palestinian nationalism after its devastation in 1948. The rhetoric of its constituent armed factions reflected this new stage in the Palestinian struggle.

In 1969, the Popular Front said: "To prepare the entire people for war means to create the people in arms." Fateh said: "Launching the revolution is achieved by establishing training camps, organizing popular militia and armed youth, and building a Palestinian civil defense." And, "Let our slogan for this phase be: Let the Palestinian revolution begin."[6] In 1968, the PLO National Charter was amended to reflect this new reality, saying: the armed struggle is "the only way to liberate Palestine."

The potency of the armed struggle strategy against Israel would prove brief. But for three years after the 1967 War, dozens of small-scale operations were carried out inside Israel and the Occupied Territories from across the borders with Jordan, Syria, and Lebanon. By 1971, Israel was able to successfully crack down on the young, ill-prepared freedom fighters who were operating from inside the occupied West Bank and Gaza Strip. It was during this campaign by Israel that Bernawi and the two Odeh's were captured.

Female fighters were never really a critical mass inside the resistance militias. However, in Lebanon, in the 1970s, many women became guerrillas and some were assigned dangerous missions, including the transporting of explosives and combat. A few entered the movement's lore as heroes and martyrs, for example, Dalal al-Mughrabi, the nineteen-year-old who died while leading a 22-man commando unit that hijacked an Israeli bus to force the release of Palestinian prisoners; Amineh Suleiman, who led in the defense of the Chatilla refugee camp in 1982; and Ra'ida (last name unknown), whose morale-raising voice across Fateh's wireless during the battles in 1978, 1982, and 1983 is remembered with much admiration. Abu Musa, leader of the splinter group that split with Fateh in 1983 said, "I raise my hat to Raida." (Reported in the interview with Fatima Bernawi, Tunis, Winter 1990.)

In the late 1960s, the Armed Resistance, with its locus in Jordan, was gathering strength, aided by an influx of primarily young males from the Palestinian communities in the diaspora in Jordan, Syria, Lebanon, and

Egypt. The volunteers streamed in, particularly after the celebrated battle at Karameh. On March 21, 1968, several thousand Israeli soldiers crossed the Jordan river and attacked a guerrilla concentration at this refugee village, just inside the border in Jordan. Karameh was memorable because in the fighting that ensued, a few hundred Palestinian guerrillas, assisted by the Jordanian military, fought a valiant battle that forced the Israelis to withdraw.

But then the simmering conflict over power between the Jordanian military and the guerrillas rose to the surface, erupting into full-fledged battles during the period 1970–1971. In retrospect, the Palestinian-Jordanian confrontation appears to have been inevitable as the Jordanian regime could hardly have tolerated an armed camp in its midst. The breach, however, was accelerated by elements within the Palestinian resistance who engaged in provocative rhetoric and activities that were threatening to the Hashemite regime. Foremost bearer of radicalism among the factions was the Popular Front, which called for revolution against the traditional "bourgeois" and "reactionary" regimes all over the Middle East. The battles of the Jordanian civil war were fought mostly in Amman and the nearby refugee camps, which were the hub of the resistance and thus suffered severe bombardment by the Jordanian military. Peace finally arrived through the mediation of Jamal Abdel Nasser, president of Egypt, who brokered a peace agreement whereby the PLO agreed to move its operations permanently out of Jordan.[7]

In retrospect, we now know that Fateh leaders, the men who spearheaded the armed resistance movement, had no illusions that the Palestinians alone could muster a potent military force, one that could be victorious against Israel. What Arafat and his colleagues had hoped would happen was that the Palestinian commando operations would edge the Arab countries to unite—a necessary condition if the Palestinians were ever to get a state in Palestine.[8]

The Armed Resistance, however, had burst Palestine political silence, unleashing revolutionary rhetoric, posters, and banners. The kaffiyeh, the Arab male headdress, became especially synonymous with the image of the Palestinian militant—both the male and the female. The kaffiyeh thus was transformed from its mundane purpose of protection from extreme weather to a political symbol invoking pride and danger.

The kaffiyeh-covered faces of Palestinian freedom fighters brought to Western consciousness the image of terrorism, especially after the airline hijackings by militants from the Popular Front and the violence at the Munich Olympics. (Much later, in the 1980s, however, the kaffiyeh became fashionable to wear in the metropolitan centers of the West.) In the Palestinian and Arab communities, the kaffiyeh-clad militants were called *fida'yyin* (masculine) and *fida'iyat* (feminine), literally meaning individuals who were willing to sacrifice their lives for the cause—and if killed, their mothers were revered and called "mothers of martyrs."[9]

Among the children, militants were given the name lion cubs for the boys (*ashbal*) and flowers for the girls (*zahrat*). These were the adolescents, shown by the media, who wore fatigues while training in militia camps or marching in formation for the Revolution.

The leading Fateh women had to consider their place in the young armed struggle movement, in the cadre organization, and in the militia, being raised in camps in Jordan, Syria, and Lebanon. In 1968, Fateh's militia camps were crowded with enthusiastic young men but young female supporters had nowhere to go. Fateh was far behind the smaller Popular Front that not only opened its membership to women but had mixed-gender camps as well. Fateh did not officially admit women to its ranks until 1970, two years after the matter was raised by Um Jihad and decided upon at Fateh's first General Congress.

Fateh insider Um Jihad decided early on not to have a separate women's organization in Fateh, which probably would have meant being outside the main cadre organization and having little chance of reaching high leadership posts. (Fateh's organization consisted of a hierarchy of cells, areas, regions—generally referred to as country-level units—the General Congress, the Revolutionary Council, and the Central Committee.)

Um Jihad's position was:

> for women to participate in the regional leadership and for the women's sector to be part of the areas—not keep it separate as women. They should be represented in the local leadership and for the women's sector to be under the local leadership—just as the men's sector.

She said she "succeeded in this vision and each region now has women leaders." Only in 1990, however, did a female—Um Jihad—finally gain a seat in Fateh's top Central Committee.

The immediate matter that needed the attention of the women's leadership in Fateh was the need to set up camps for the young women who showed up in Syria and Jordan for militia training. Fateh's leadership had promised to open women's camps early in 1968, but no action had taken place by the time a top Fateh meeting was held in Damascus that year. The meeting was held at Um and Abu Lutuf's house in Damascus and was attended by Arafat; attending from the women's leadership were Um Jihad, Abu Khadra, and Um Lutuf.

This is how Abu Khadra remembers it. She said:

We told them what is the difference between us and you. Is it in the effort? To be committed to our cause and leave other matters aside is more difficult for the woman because she leaves the comforts of the home and has to stand up to the restrictive barrier created by her family.

She then said:

That was our question: We want to understand why do you discriminate against us? Everyone of you knows us here in front of you. Are we not committed? In the first place we have difficulties as it is and, in the second, we see that our movement does not believe in the struggle of the woman. Is the woman, in the final analysis, a fragile flower that is only an image in this movement or is she an indivisible part of the popular revolution?

Arafat's response was to move that the matter be discussed separately, at another time with Abu Lutuf, who was in charge of Fateh's cadre organization. The meeting that followed with Abu Lutuf set the tone for how women would participate in the Fateh-dominated PLO.

Abu Khadra recalls that Abu Lutuf, after a very long discussion, concluded with this. "He said: You take the initiative, you work, and then you will reap from your hard work. The work is going to last a long time and this is a cause of the woman and the man." Abu Lutuf's words echoed Fateh's general philosophy of a political leadership that favors political entrepreneurship over strict cadre organization. "Even for the brothers, it (women's participation) became a natural matter," Abu Khadra concluded, and, as if to waive any doubts, she added, "We deal with the brothers in an objective manner."

Later in the year, the first Fateh light-arms training camp for young women opened, and Arafat attended the graduation ceremonies and gave trophies to the graduating young women. Other training camps in Syria and Jordan followed during the period 1968–1969. But the role of the armed woman was an exaggerated one that reflected little how the bulk of women in fact participated.[10]

Social relief, the mainstay of women's work, and the female cadres' drive to mobilize the women in the refugee camps were nowhere to be seen in the imagery of heroism of the Palestinian National Movement. It was an invisibility that would continue to haunt the women's leadership throughout the history of the national liberation struggle. And yet, women's participation was an important part of the Palestinian nation-building, which was especially focused inside the refugee camps. Recruitment of the camp's young men and women was clearly a central domestic strategy of the PLO.

IV.

The role of women in the Palestinian movement is symbolized in the text of the PLO's Revised (1968) National Charter:

> That there is a Palestinian community and that it has material, spiritual and historical connections with Palestine are indisputable facts. It is a national duty to bring up individual Palestinians in an Arab revolutionary manner. All means of information and education must be adopted in order to acquaint the Palestinian with his country in the most profound manner possible, both spiritual and material. He must be prepared for the armed struggle and ready to sacrifice his wealth and his life in order to win back his homeland and bring about its liberation.

The Charter thus asked no less than a fundamental change in how Palestinians thought of themselves as a people: to replace national despair and disillusionment with pride and unity of purpose. And women's community organizing inside the refugee camps was to be a crucial aspect of that journey.

The refugee camps were natural environments for the recruitment of women and men to the armed struggle organizations, for the refugees stood stark in their alienation, powerlessness, and poverty. In Jordan, the Palestinian population spread throughout its major cities and towns, but there are also thousands who still lived in refugee camps. There are some eleven refugee camps in Jordan. Five date back to 1948 and are administered by UNRWA. These are: Zarka, Irbid, and Madaba, named after nearby host cities, and Wehdat and Jabal Hussein, near Amman. Six new camps: Talbiyeh, Jarash, Baqa', Suf, al-Azmi al-Mufti, and Hittin were set up in 1968 to house about 80,000 of the 200,000 refugees from the 1967 War.[11]

The question of Palestinian identity in Jordan is particularly poignant and complicated by the fact that there is a vast economic chasm between those from the middle class who found a comfortable home in Jordan and the largely rural and poor refugee camp residents. The class of merchants, professionals, and government officials have developed a stake in the Jordanian system and were bound to be politically cautious. (Amman's old town commercial center, noted for its gold jewelry markets, was built by this class who came mainly from the refugee wave of 1948.) To residents of the refugee camps, allegiance to the Jordanian regime was a much harder task to achieve, for their desperate surroundings defined Palestinian uprootedness and statelessness.

The Palestinian refugee camps have never had an economic base, with just a few grocery and repair shops. The old village chiefs were still considered the local leaders, but everyone knew that they were powerless and that new men were in charge. Apart from UNRWA, which provided social services to the Palestinian refugees, the camps were controlled by the internal intelligence and security services. Their names were familiar to Palestinians: *al-mukhabarat* in the Arab countries—and specific to Lebanon, *squad ten* and *deuzieme bureau*; and, in Israel, the *shin bet* and the security apparatus associated with the occupation administration in the West Bank and Gaza Strip.

PLO ambassador Shahid performed political work in a refugee camp when she was a young student in Lebanon. She said the Armed Resistance found a dual social reality in the refugee camps' social networks. On the one hand, she said:

> The village was gone, the neighborhood was gone, the clan and the tribe were gone. Every reference was gone. There was a great deal of rejection of political organizations that failed in 1948. The idea was to build new political frameworks that are more suitable to people's wants and desires.

At the same time, family networks survived and Shahid said they served the movement well:

> The national movement is practically the product of the camps. The Palestinian revolution is a product of the refugees in the Palestinian society—be they in the (West) Bank, in Gaza (Strip), in Lebanon, or in Jordan. Between this society of refugees and its leadership is a direct relationship. That is, the leadership of this organization (PLO) came from the refugee camps. Abu Iyad, Abu Ammar and others, maybe they came from other places but they are originally children of the camps through their families.

She further explained:

> There are connections so that sometimes in the same family there are (members) from the Democratic and Popular fronts and Fateh. It is possible to have in the same family four sisters in four factions so that communication is natural and familial. There is a kind of communication that is difficult to express in political science terms, something that is nearly spiritual.

The refugee camp was a new world to the women's leadership that existed at the fringes of their comfortable, middle-class lives. The older generations of women from the camps were poor and illiterate villagers who had little chance to step outside their neighborhoods or their gender-segregated social existence. Their daughters fared somewhat better, receiving education at UNRWA schools (through middle school and sometimes, when available secondary school). By 1963, girls and women were one-third of the UNRWA school population. Still, women from the camps found jobs mostly as seamstresses, seasonal agricultural workers, or house cleaners. Some, among the more educated, became elementary school teachers who journeyed as far as the oil-rich Gulf countries and Libya for employment.[12]

But there were cultural norms that prevailed in the Palestinian refugee camps and in the Jordanian society alike. In these socially conservative communities, young marriage-age Palestinian women could find themselves under the watchful eyes of the family so that their honor could be closely guarded. Every young woman learns early on not to be out in public at night, not to associate freely with men, and to dress conservatively. Palestinian women also share the Arab norm of *sit beit* (the lady of the house). The wife and mother is expected to faithfully cook time-consuming meals, manage her house and children's lives, and attend to common social obligations. The life of the female can be tightly bound to the cycles of birth, marriage, sickness, and death.

Making initial contacts with the women in the camps followed familiar rituals. The visitors would arrive unannounced—as was the custom—and would begin by delivering the proper greetings and polite inquiry about the children and the household in general. They would be offered and would accept a cup of Arabic coffee (served strong and sweet in a small cup) and they would likely be asked to stay on for a meal. The hostess might understandably have been wary of the organizers, but her nationalist sentiments were indeed indisputable.

One of the earliest lessons learned from encounters between members of the women's leadership and women living in the refugee camps was the great depth of nationalist sentiment that these ordinary women had. Certainly it matched that of the politicos and even surpassed it. Um Nasser made this discovery when she began to visit the camps near Amman to deliver small financial allowances to families of martyred freedom fighters. She said she heard it in the grateful answer of an old woman who had just lost a twenty-year-old son in the fighting. The woman had said: "I, take an allowance? I am the one who wants to participate and sweat to pay you."

Jehan Helou, who was one of Fateh's leading cadres in Lebanon during that period, reiterated what Um Nasser said. Helou's first awakening to the determination and bravery of women living in the camps occurred at the time of the 1969 refugee camps' uprising in Lebanon. Throughout Lebanon, camp residents had staged two months of protests and demonstrations against the tight control of the Lebanese intelligence and security forces. Camp residents, with the help of sympathetic Lebanese, drove the Lebanese authorities out of the camps and then organized local committees that took charge of their own internal civil affairs. Helou recollected the participation of women:

> I saw it with my own eyes in 1969 when women in the camps—when the Lebanese army attacked—they faced the tanks. . . . ordinary women and probably illiterate. And they were not organized; there weren't any cadres at that time anyway. I mean, that shows how deep is the national issue inside the woman.

During the period 1968–1969, the women's leadership—whether at the Women's Union or working for the factions—was basically a formless group of activists with little in the shape of organization or agenda. Their initial inroads into the refugee camp society occurred in Jordan (and to some extent Syria); these were tentative steps, cut short by the Jordanian civil war during the period 1970–1971. However, those women's initiatives eventually became the basis for Fateh's social welfare policy—and the PLO's after Fateh took control of that organization. The projects in which women took leading roles were Um Jihad's Families of the Martyrs foundation and Samed (acronym for Palestine Martyrs Works Society—literally meaning steadfast), which was started by Um Nasser. Samed eventually evolved into the PLO's economic institution (more on that later). The PLO's health arm, the Palestinian Red Crescent Society, was founded in 1968 by Arafat's brother, Fathi.

V.

The first social welfare project in the Palestinian National Movement was started by Fateh in 1965, just as the group was emerging from its clandestine existence. The idea was to distribute allowances (from then rather meager funds) to the families of men killed in commando raids on Israel. In 1965, the structure of the project was simply a committee of three, Um Jihad and two men—Samih Darwish, who continued to work with Um Jihad as the executive director of her institution at the headquarters in Amman, and Ribhi Awad, who seems to have gone into political oblivion.

Um Jihad explained that:

> Beside the financial, social, health, and educational care, it was very important that the family of the martyr, when it loses its father or son, doesn't break the spiritual connection. The most important issue is the symbolic one: to connect families of the martyrs with the Revolution.

Um Jihad's Families of the Martyrs foundation was born from this humble beginning and, by the mid-1980s, it had grown into a bona fide social welfare organization with the largest budget in the PLO (over U.S. $100 million in 1990). Several months after our interview, however, Um Jihad's institution lost, as did the rest of the PLO, a great deal of its funding that previously came from Saudi Arabia, Kuwait, and the United Arab Emirates. The Gulf states were angered by the PLO's sympathies with Iraq, which had occupied Kuwait in the summer of 1990. Afterwards, Um Jihad said, the financial situation of the Families of the Martyrs foundation became very tenuous as funds arrived in a much more unpredictable manner, and the competition for funds among various PLO agencies became more intense.

The headquarters of the Families of the Martyrs foundation, which was moved in the mid-1980s from Damascus to Amman, resemble any governmental welfare office. In 1990, its three-story building in Amman was the base for some seventy-five employees, mainly women drawn from families of the martyrs; it contained specialized bureaus and offices and a room filled with new computers to handle the increased demand for aid after the start of the 1987 Intifada in the Occupied Territories. Crowding the waiting room were women and men who had travelled from Jordan, the West Bank, or elsewhere to see the chief of the organization Um Jihad about some financial need or health problem. Um Jihad was proud to say her program "was a first of its kind in world revolutions. Even from the Iranian revolution when it began, they came to learn from our experience," she said.

I asked if the policy to support these families was one she herself had suggested. "Oh yes," she said, "my role had a great deal of influence in addition to the general policies of the PLO." She illustrated this by pointing to the decision about who should receive the funding allowances that Fateh distributed. It was a practical step that was also revolutionary, for it broke with the Arab tradition of how income was controlled. Um Jihad explained:

> In relation to wife of the martyr, we decided internally in the institution that wife of the martyr will care for her children and be the guardian. As you know, with the laws (of Islam), the guardian may be the father of the husband or uncle of the children. We refused this condition and supported the tie of the mother to her children, that she be guardian and responsible for them. This helped a lot in solving family conflicts.

Interest in empowering women through economic means was also evident in the modest genesis of Samed during the period 1968–1969, the

PLO's economic arm. Um Nasser was one of its pioneers who began Fateh's vocational training classes for women in Jordan. The first classes were held at Fateh House in Jabal Hussein, one of ten mountains where, in 1970, the 520,000 population of Amman lived. There were literacy, sewing, and typing classes; political lectures were also offered about the Palestinian problem and Fateh's goals and strategies.

Um Nasser said the house also doubled as a meeting place for "the brothers"—Arafat and the other Fateh leaders. She said, "They told us this is Fateh House; you can come and work as a women's sector. You can call it your *tanzim* (cadre organization) house. So I went and took charge of the house."

Um Nasser also arranged for light-weapons training for women who were also held at Fateh House. Did she actually fight, I asked. "Of course," she answered:

> There were clashes [with the Jordanian forces] near Salt in Jordan and we used to fight. I mean, I used to stand guard till morning. There were very difficult times. Sometimes, when I would go to one of our brother fighters and tell him give me the gun because it is time for my guard duty, he would find it very hard to give it to a sister. Afterwards, they passed beyond that complex and we became part of them.

Numerous Palestinian young women eventually trained in the militia and took part in the armed resistance, but among Um Nasser's generation, this was a true rarity. However, as life became more dangerous for Um Nasser, it also became more meaningful and fulfilling. "I started my real life when I committed to Fateh because I found the way that makes it possible for me to actualize myself," she explained.

Women's vocational workshops and adult literacy classes were the mainstay of women's mobilization. Every group on the scene— the different factions and the Women's Union, which in the 1960s was held by the charitable societies and Fateh—had their own vocational and literacy classes. The distinction between what Fateh women did and what the Women's Union did was quite hazy from that period. In reality, the institutional distinctions that evolved later in Lebanon between the Families of the Martyrs foundation, Samed (Fateh's vocational and production programs), and the Women's Union were just beginning to take shape in 1971.

Educational workshops were generally held at centers in the refugee camps, operated by the individual factions or the Women's Union; these were small-scale operations that occupied one or two rooms with very little in the way of equipment. Funding was modest, coming mainly from membership fees and voluntary contributions. Funds were also generated from women's crafts bazaars, which were held during religious holidays such as Christmas and al-Fitr, the Muslim feast celebrated at the end of the fasting month of Ramadan.

To Women's Union president Abdel Hadi, socialized in the tradition of the women's charitable societies, vocational training had a fundamentally social benefit. "In regards to what relates to the woman, it is very important for us to train her for a respectable life, for an independent life," she said, "I mean, we had many vocational centers in the camps." The Women's Union had fourteen of these centers, mostly in Jordan, by 1971.

Behind its placid front, however, the women's vocational center was essentially a political enterprise, an outpost of the Armed Resistance in the refugee camp. Ghazi Khalili, who wrote one of the first studies on female Palestinian militants, explained the reasoning behind the focus on vocational training for women:

> The vocational center was the hub for organizing. This is the method which dealt with the family's rejection of the young woman's going out of the house. The Palestinian family, even at that time, was generally against the young woman joining the Revolution. While joining the vocational center to train for a profession would be met with encouragement from the family. . . . This way the Revolution entered the Palestinian home.[13]

Um Nasser said the vocational center was a pragmatic strategy that served the individual woman and the national movement alike. She said:

> These centers, you know, the leadership found very serious and positive. First of all the young women who learned typing were able to find work. We used to take them and employ them in the offices of the Revolution: in public information, in the office of mobilization, and in the office of the PLO. They benefitted from these young women. At the same time, it lightened the burden of having to pay them because when the young woman would get out and get sewing lessons and become a seamstress, we would give her a sewing machine and she can stay home and work. Now they acquired self-sufficiency.

Toward the end of the Jordanian period of the Palestinian movement, and as it was preparing to relocate to Lebanon, the question that presented itself to Fateh's leadership was this: What should be the future of its mushrooming vocational training programs? Um Nasser's vision for Samed was that it be dedicated to the preservation and development of

Palestinian folklore—with she as its cultural ambassador. Abu Ala', who was also on the committee in charge of Fateh's vocational projects, was an economist by training and had a different plan. He wanted to build economic enterprises that could generate funds for the faction. A project that turned out affordable uniforms for the fighters already existed at Tal el-Za'tar refugee camp near Beirut, and it was an example of what Abu Ala' had in mind. (Abu Ala' is the man who represented the PLO at the secret negotiations in Norway in 1993, which produced the Israeli-PLO accord, otherwise known as the Declaration of Principles that formed the basis for starting official negotiations between the two sides.)

The conflict between Abu Ala' and Um Nasser over Samed's mission accelerated once the Armed Resistance moved to Lebanon during the period 1971–1972, and it was during that time that Arafat asked Um Nasser to head his office. She summed up the exchange she had with Arafat in this way:

> I went to brother Abu Ammar and said that it is me who started these projects and I disagree with brother Abu Ala'. He said: What do you want with it, leave the matter to him. What you did all these years, the accomplishments, the vocational centers, will not be forgotten. What I need is a head of my office. I have no filing cabinet or office, nothing—and, in fact, Abu Ammar never stayed in one place. He said here take the first, this file. I said: This is it? He said this is the first file. Take my papers. He said be with me as head of my office.

Um Nasser accepted Arafat's offer and was in charge of his office (called the General Commander Office) until his retirement in 1986—when she began supervising the headquarters of the Women's Union in Tunis.

In review, what the leading female cadre did during the Jordanian period appears to have departed little from time-tested activities of the charitable societies—though now accompanied by openly nationalist messages. The women's leadership was comprised of operatives who faithfully carried out tasks given to them by the top male leadership. Regardless, the individual initiatives of these women pioneers served to establish some of the first footholds of the Resistance among the girl and women residents of the refugee camps. Furthermore, in the 1970s in Lebanon, these small pilot projects evolved into the backbone of the PLO's social welfare policy and grew to encompass thousands of employees and volunteers.

VI.

The dominant model for women's participation in the Palestinian National Movement was caretaking, which greatly concerned the leftists from the second generation, women like Laila Khaled of the Popular Front, Nihaya Muhammad of the Democratic Front, and Jihan Helou and Khadijeh Abu Ali of Fateh. These were self-professed political and social revolutionaries who wanted the Women's Union, to take on the agenda of social change for women. They were critical of the inherent conservatism of the Women's Union which only offered a "bourgeois" kind of liberation. They thought the line separating charitable work from revolutionary work was transparently thin.

The young leftists, who later led the Union in Lebanon in the 1970s, were dissatisfied with the centrists from the older generations who saw women's liberation as a by-product of national development—not requiring special focus. Indeed, expressed in the words of Abdel Hadi, the women's leadership from the first generation believed that, "First we seek equality with all other nations in the world—self determination. This we lack. Afterwards, work for the equality for men and women in rights and obligations."

Helou and her colleagues learned quickly from their participation in cadre work that belief in national liberation did not necessarily translate to a more progressive attitude regarding women. Helou never forgot the remark of one of the comrades. She said he "was very kind but very backward and he used to laugh at me. (He said) 'imagine she wants to work for the liberation of Palestine and also liberate women,'—as if this is something shocking or a joke."

Popular Front's Khaled felt the same way as Helou and thought attention should be placed on educating the males in the Armed Resistance. Both the Popular Front and the Democratic Front, which split from the Popular Front in 1969, were on record as supporting the equality of the sexes—but their stance was mainly theoretical and based on class not gender analysis.[14]

Later, Abu Ali would write about those early years in Jordan, saying, "The woman faces her family responsibilities and those toward her nation alone, as if her problem is solely hers."[15] In 1990, she would reiterate that conclusion, adding that not much has changed in the status of women in the Palestinian movement.

The inescapable conclusion at the end of the brief Jordanian period was that the vast majority of Palestinian women remained politically unorganized because of social restrictions regarding their behavior. The young leftists thought the Palestinian movement must address the special situation of women. In the words of a cadre of the Democratic Front, "We should provide conditions and requirements to put the female public at the depth [center] of the general strategy of the Revolution, militarily, politically and organizationally."[16] If we just promote the traditional roles, these women from the second generation asked, how will we be able to become full participants—as promised by the PLO National Charter?[17]

The intellectual discourse among the leading women and men about strategies to increase the participation of women in the national movement never penetrated to the ground in the refugee camps. For ordinary women and men, the symbols of the movement were the leaders of the factions, Arafat and the rest: the guerrillas seen at their posts and driving around in their jeeps proudly displaying their weapons; the athletic center where the boys and young men congregated; the women's center; the revolutionary leaflets and occasional political lectures; and the funeral procession for the martyrs. In the end, the leftists learned how difficult it was to plan beyond extending a few services to the refugees, especially when the national movement was consumed with recurrent violent crises.

VII.

In the last days of the Palestinian movement in Jordan, Um Nasser was seen fighting in the bloody battle between the Jordanian and Palestinian forces that raged in September 1970 in and around Amman. In Palestinian history, Black September (namesake of the terrorist group) was so named for the heavy bombardment and savagery that was inflicted on the civilian populations in the refugee camps, especially Jabal Hussein and Wehdat, at the outskirts of the city.

At the end of September 1970, longtime champion of the Palestinian cause Jamal Abdel Nasser, of Egypt, died of a heart attack. In November, Ba'athist Hafez Assad took the helm in Syria, establishing a tighter control of the country and the Palestinian refugee camps within it. In July 1971, another round of battles was fought in Jordan in Ajlun and Jarash, and by October 1971, the Palestinian resistance was finished there.

Gone were all its visible structures: the militias, the offices, and the social centers in the refugee camps. Fateh House, which housed Um Nasser's first projects, was one of the first casualties. Afterwards, as part of the rapprochement between Arafat and King Hussein, it was agreed that PLO organizing inside Jordan would be prohibited.[18]

The refugee camps were reoccupied by the Jordanian forces. They are now administered by either UNRWA (the 1948 camps) or the Department of Palestinian Affairs at the Jordanian Foreign Ministry (the 1967 camps), with their basic services connected to the networks of nearby cities. In

1990, the number of Palestinians in Jordan who carried refugee identification cards totaled 916,000; of those, only 270,136 still live in the camps.

By 1973, the PLO and its women's leadership was headquartered in Beirut, close to Sabra and Chatilla refugee camps. Palestinian militias were already in Lebanon, but were reinforced by remnants of the guerrilla units that arrived from Jordan. (As agreed upon in the Nasser-brokered Cairo Agreement of November 1969, the Palestinian forces established new bases in the south of Lebanon and to the east in the Biqa' Valley.) Several of the younger women, such as Sayigh and Abu Ali, made the trek with the PLO to Lebanon. For Um Nasser, the move to Lebanon was personally pivotal; as head of Arafat's new office, she was now close to the center of PLO decision-making.

All those who led the women's mobilizational effort during the Jordanian period survived the Jordanian civil war and continued their commitment to the Palestinian cause. Most, however, lived away from the new hub of the movement in Lebanon. Abu Khadra and Um Lutuf lived in Kuwait and Egypt respectively. Abu Khadra remained active in Fateh, in its Kuwaiti branch leadership. She also became involved in the educational field by founding and heading a school for Palestinian children named Dar al-Hanan al-Ahliya. Um Lutuf stayed in the secretariat until 1974, when she withdrew from mobilizational work, saying the Women's Union had become elitist and its leadership entrenched. But she continued in Fateh and worked for many years at the Arab League's Palestine office in Cairo and later in Tunis (retiring after the League returned to Cairo). Um Lutuf eventually landed a seat in Fateh's Revolutionary Council (the interim policymaking body between the faction's General Congress and its top Central Committee). The other politically active wife of a top Fateh leader, Um Jihad, continued in her role as leader of the Families of the Martyrs foundation, and also worked inside Fateh's cadre organization, rising to its Revolutionary Council and, finally, to its highest Central Committee.

As a caveat, it is important to mention that most factional and PLO official positions are best considered rewards of long-term service and loyalty, rather than indications of power or specialized functions or responsibilities. This is not to say that Um Lutuf and Um Jihad did not have important roles in the Palestinian movement. Um Jihad's leadership in the social welfare arena, for example, is undeniable. Their influence, however, should be seen as primarily informal through their connection to Fateh leaders. In any case, these women gained a great deal of practical political education and savvy. It is knowledge that is difficult to demonstrate in the environment of secrecy, turf protection, and a general tendency to keep a lid on things in the PLO's cadre organizations.

In Lebanon, however, the realm of the women's leadership became more institutionalized in the Women's Union. Its president, Abdel Hadi, remained in Amman to preside over the Union from a distance, but made regular commutes to Beirut. (She told me a big difficulty she encountered in her work was the fact that she never lived close to union headquarters.) However, it was the younger leftists from the second generation (who lived mainly in Beirut) who took charge of the union.

Chapter 3

BEIRUT
National Mobilization and Civil War

I.

In Lebanon, during the period 1971–1982, the Palestinian women's leadership experienced its greatest success in the Palestinian diaspora but also its longest, although intermittent, subjection to conditions of warfare and civil strife. The Lebanese period in the history of the Palestinian National Movement, which was marked by waves of nation-building and destruction, began with *al-mad al-thawri* (the revolutionary expansion) years of 1971–1974, when the refugee camps enthusiastically welcomed the Resistance forces coming from Jordan. However, from 1974 to 1989, Lebanon was mired in civil war and invasions. Beirut ceased being the hub of the Palestinian movement in 1982, when Israeli forces crossed into Lebanon, marched into the city, and forced the PLO to leave. The PLO's headquarters eventually moved to Tunis, which then hosted the Arab League. Tunis also became the home of Fateh's leadership, while Damascus became the center of the Popular and Democratic fronts.[1]

From 1974 to the Palestinian exodus from Beirut, women's organizing occurred under the specter of the unpredictable violence that erupted sporadically across the country and from air bombardment by the Israeli Air Force. The long term structural problem was the fragility of the Lebanese political system, which was established according to the principle of sectarianism. Maronite/Muslim distribution of power followed roughly a 5:6 ratio in parliamentary seats (now it is 5:5). The presidency belonged to a Maronite, while other leadership posts were distributed to the other sects. The rise of the Palestinian movement, the arrival of the leadership from Jordan, and the consequent heating up of the Israeli-Lebanese border hastened the unravelling of Lebanon's sectarian power

51

arrangement. The Lebanese civil war, which began in 1975, continued beyond the PLO's exit in 1982, engulfing much of the Lebanese and Palestinian populations. The initial battles were between rightist militias that represented Christian Maronite interests, and the Palestinian militias, who had remobilized in Lebanon after exiting Jordan. Allied with the Palestinians were the Arab nationalists and leftists, mainly from the Lebanese Muslim community, who competed for power with the Maronites. In 1976, the Syrian army drove its tanks into Lebanon, ending the initial stage of the violence. Afterwards, the Syrian army, the Israelis, and Iranian volunteers from the Islamic Revolution joined the fighting, further complicating the situation.

Khadijeh Abu Ali, member of the PLO's Women's Union secretariat since 1974, said of that era:

> I remember that we built together a stone over a stone, a woman over a woman, a program over a program. Sometimes, we used to say that twenty-four hours were not enough, that the day should be thirty hours, so we can rest for a few hours.

Indeed, the phrase "the Palestinian women's leadership" (*qiyadat al-mar'a al-filastiniya*) became truly established in the culture of the Palestinian movement during its years in Lebanon. It is the "we" in Abu Ali's statement—the core of women leaders who, amidst their partisan differences, arrived at a collective identity as the political voice of the Palestinian woman. It was a voice developed by leading women's mobilization in Lebanon and speaking for the Palestinian cause in international forums.

The Palestinian forces began to arrive from Jordan in 1970, after the bombardment of the refugee camps there. By 1973, the leadership had settled in the Fakahani district of Beirut, less than 100 km from the Lebanese-Israeli border. The Women's Union headquarters was first housed in an apartment in Fakahani and later moved to the nearby Abu Shaker Street.

The symbolism of Fakahani's location could not have been more poignant; it had the promise of a bustling section of Beirut but adjacent to it was a large concentration of Palestinian refugees and poor Lebanese. Fakahani is a mixed commercial and residential area of multistory buildings in predominantly Muslim West Beirut. A short walk southeast are the Chatilla and Sabra refugee camps that housed a population of some 35,000 Palestinians and poor Lebanese. To the southwest is Beirut International Airport, which used to be one of the busiest airports in the Middle East; to the west is the Arab University, a longtime center of political activism, and further west is the Mediterranean coast; to the northwest is Abu Shaker Street, where the Women's Union headquarters was located; and to the east is the Martyrs cemetery.

The Palestinian women's leadership at Fakahani was an energetic and determined group of five or so young leftists, in their mid-20s to mid-30s, most of whom were not from Beirut. They were a new breed in the second generation who rose to leadership not via family connections but through the ranks of their respective factions. Almost all were university graduates, and their activism dated back to their student years. Most married late, delaying the responsibilities of child care. All were full-time politicos, some dividing their time between union activities and working for other PLO operations—mainly in the media operations of the Resistance, like the Institute of Palestine Studies.

Fateh's leftist contingent in the Women's Union secretariat was Mai Sayigh and Abu Ali, who came with the Resistance from Jordan, and Jihan Helou, who was in Fateh's underground in Lebanon. Helou was previously the president of the Women's Union branch in Lebanon—her sister Shadia would occupy this position later. The Democratic Front was represented by Nihaya Muhammad and the Popular Front by former commando Laila Khaled. The Iraqi Ba'ath affiliate Arab Liberation Front was first represented by Najla Nusair Bashur and, after 1977, by Wedad Ahmad, after her husband became general secretary of the Front. (She came on board in 1980 at the Third Congress of the Women's Union.)

The women's leadership in the Jordanian period remained active, albeit from a distance. President Abdel Hadi often commuted from Amman and Salwa Abu Khadra led the Union's second largest and most affluent branch in Kuwait until 1980, when she joined the secretariat. Um Lutuf left the Union in 1974, but remained well-connected inside the Palestinian movement via her husband, Fateh leader Abu Lutuf.

Um Jihad presided over her fast-growing foundation, the Families of the Martyrs, from its headquarters in Syria. Um Jihad's involvement in the Women's Union was informal and continued to be minimal. She was, however, the strategically well-placed friend who could be called upon to help when needed.

A member of the second generation, young Um Sabri joined the secretariat in 1974. She lost her Fateh commander-husband during the fighting in Jordan and was left with the responsibility of raising her children alone, which made her involvement rather tenuous. Abu Khadra, Um Sabri, and Um Nasser formed the centrist block that consistently backed Arafat. Um Nasser, however, restricted her responsibilities to publicity because, she said, "of my position at the office of brother Abu Ammar (Arafat), it was easier for me to work in publicity."

Um Nasser began working for Arafat several months after arriving in Lebanon in 1972. From Jordan, she had first gone to Cairo, sent to supervise a PLO-operated women's dormitory for students attending Cairo universities from the West Bank and Gaza Strip. After about a year in Cairo, Fateh's financial chief Abu Mazen asked her to come to Lebanon to rejuvenate Samed, the faction's vocational program—which she did, heading Samed's administrative council until moving on to set up Arafat's office. It was not until the late 1970s, however, that women again occupied leadership roles in Samed. Two women joined its administrative council, a young Ph.D. in economics and Samed's political officer.

For a woman to head the office of a national leader, and a military commander at that, was unprecedented in Arab society. Um Nasser initially did the work single-handedly, which was of course quite exhausting, but later brought *shabab* (literally young men but refers to male cadres) to help. It was also exhilarating work. Of Arafat's now well-known schedule she said:

> Brother Abu Ammar is always on the go; he rests two to three hours at night and a half hour during the day . . . fifteen years of wars and struggling. Staying up. I would start from nine in the morning and I would not know when it is day and when it is night.

For over two decades, Um Nasser was considered Arafat's First Lady, attending to some of the ceremonial functions of his office. For example, she said:

> He would send me outside on his behalf to pay a visit to the prime minister's wife when she was sick, to visit Camille Chamoun (former president of Lebanon) when he had an eye operation. Go take him flowers. Social functions like that.

Um Nasser has the presence of one who could easily have been a Middle Eastern queen from an earlier time, when palace intrigue was the order of the day. But what her words portrayed in our interview in 1990 was absolute loyalty to the Palestinian cause and to Arafat. Her past power was vivid in the words of her Tunisian driver, who spoke as one who had shared in her moments of glory: "You should have seen her then, how the men would react to her." She acknowledged the centrality of her position when she told me with a faint smile, "I was at the office of the General Commander. I was in the political kitchen."

II.

The period of "the revolutionary expansion" was filled with promise, and all signs indicated that the people living in the refugee camps were receptive and ready. In the camps, popular committees, formed in the aftermath of the 1969 camp uprising, supervised an unprecedented pace of development.[2] Building projects were booming, bomb shelters were being built, and potholes were fixed. The Palestinian revolution rose above ground with health clinics, women and youth activities. And militia and civil defense training became available.

The living situation of the Palestinian refugees in Lebanon was more desperate than it was in Jordan, in that a much larger proportion lived inside camps that were no more than shanty towns; the rest lived in cities and towns, mostly in Beirut and the southern towns of Tyre and Sidon. In 1975, over half of the 350,000 Palestinians registered as refugees with UNRWA lived in fifteen UNRWA camps (now twelve), and a few unofficial ones like the Sabra camp. These were the descendants of the 100,000 Palestinians who crossed the Lebanese border in 1948 from their homes in Galilee and the Haifa provinces of northern Palestine.[3] The refugee camps dotted the Lebanese landscape mainly along the western coastal areas, from Nahr al-Barid and Badawi camps near Tripoli in the north, to Rashidiya near Tyre in the south; one camp, Wavell, was located near Ba'albak, to the east of Mount Lebanon, in the Biqa' Valley.

The camps were under strict control of the ever-present Lebanese intelligence and security services until 1969, when residents successfully forced them to leave. UNRWA tried to mute the difficult condition of the refugees by providing education for the children and caring for some of the other basic infrastructural needs. The post-uprising atmosphere was such a departure from the previous twenty years that it caused many to pause and exercise caution.

Um Nasser experienced some of that tentativeness firsthand when Arafat sent her to do civil defense training at the Sabra camp. She said he sent her to shame the men who were reluctant to join the militia. "He wanted to prove that here is my office chief and a sister who had come to train in front of you."

Lebanon held promise for the Resistance because it was a more open social and political environment than the desert kingdom of Jordan. Beirut was a busy international trading and banking center and a hub of the Arab intellectual movement. It was also a place of political intrigue, fed by a rich pool of political forces and ideologies: the Maronites, the Druz, the Sunnis, and the Shiites, each in turn diverging in fluid battle lines between competing Lebanese family dynasties. The Palestinian movement brought into focus the serious structural problems of the sectarianism that was embedded in the Lebanese political system itself. Lebanese politics was a deep hole out of which the Palestinians could not climb.

But in the beginning, the Resistance found a hospitable political environment among Palestinians and Lebanese alike. The polls from the early 1970s showed that most of the Lebanese were supportive of the Palestinian cause, and thousands took to the streets in demonstrations of solidarity.[4] In the women's arena, Palestinian women worked in the charitable societies, together with women from notable Lebanese families, to set up the first vocational training workshops in the refugee camps. Maintaining friendships with the Lebanese women was a deliberate decision, said a Fateh cadre who participated in that work, a tactic meant to maintain their support.

At the secretariat of the Women's Union, however, things were in disarray during the period of the "revolutionary expansion." There were many problems to be sorted out: having to regroup from the disaster in Jordan; a scarcity of funds to support new programs; and the fact that the leadership was divided between the official union headquarters in Cairo and the operational leadership held by the Resistance women in Beirut. Cairo had been the official seat of the union since 1966, when it moved from East Jerusalem after being banned by Jordan, which was in control of the city then. According to Jehan Helou, president of Lebanon's branch during that time, the total achievement of the union during its first few years in Lebanon was a few vocational workshops and an occasional crafts bazaar to raise funds. Therefore, there were few resources for mobilizing women.

III.

The activities of the leaders of the Women's Union picked up in 1974, as they organized the Union's Second Congress, held that year. This is the general conference of representatives of the branches that sets the policy agenda of the union, usually meeting in conjunction with the National Council if critical decisions are to be made. But, during a twenty-year period, only four such congresses were convened.

The women's congress had two major items on its agenda. One was to vote on the de facto secretariat that was now dominated by the resistance factions. The acceptance of this group was a foregone conclusion after the factions came under the PLO umbrella at the 7th National Council session in Cairo in 1970. The vote for the women's leadership was a mere formality since the formula for representation and the nominations were customarily determined in advance by the leadership of the factions. The secretariat elected in 1974 consisted of thirteen women: six from Fateh; one each from the Popular Front, Democratic Front, Popular Front-General Command, Sa'iqa, and the Arab Liberation

Front; and two independents. Fateh's control of the union was evident from the start in that it had a much larger voting strength there than in the PLO Executive Committee, where representation of the factions showed a greater equilibrium.

The other important objective of the women's congress proved to be volatile, which was why the meeting was held sooner than planned. Arafat had wanted the Palestinian mass organizations to promptly pass resolutions to show support of the PLO's new political program. The mass organizations consisted of women's and student's unions and labor and professional syndicates affiliated with the PLO. Until the 1980s, however, they were still minimally represented in the militia-dominated National Council and, therefore, their positions were learned from votes in their respective general conferences.

The new political program, known as the Provisional Solution (*al-hal al-marhali* or *al-qarar al-marhali*), or the Ten Point Program, had already been approved by the 12th National Council that met in Beirut in June of 1974. It was subsequently passed by the mass organizations, but only after a great deal of vigorous debate.

The controversial article was the second point that said:

> The PLO will struggle by every means, foremost of which is armed struggle, to liberate Palestinian land and to establish the people's national, independent and fighting authority on every part of Palestinian land to be liberated. This requires making more changes in the balance of power in favor of our people and their struggle.

This declaration was a dramatic step away from the PLO National Charter's emphasis on waging an armed struggle to liberate Palestine, as revised in 1968 (Article 9). In fact, the Provisional Solution was the predecessor to several such decisions toward a political resolution of the Palestine question. The most dramatic was in 1988, when the 19th National Council proclaimed a Palestinian state to be in the occupied West Bank and Gaza Strip. Soon after, Arafat made his famous statement in Geneva, that recognized Israel's right to exist, and renounced terrorism.

The critical phrase in the second point of the Provisional Solution was: "to establish the people's national, independent and fighting authority on every part of Palestinian land to be liberated." This, everyone in the higher circles of the Resistance knew, opened the possibility that "every part" might become "any part," that is, settling for part of Palestine for a state—in effect, the 1967 Occupied Territories, which is what was finally decided in 1988.

Arafat had maneuvered the Provisional Solution, through the 12th National Council, to situate the PLO in a better place in the international political environment of the post-1973 October War between Israel and Egypt, which set in motion the negotiations that brought about peace between the two countries. The Palestinians, Arafat argued, needed to be prepared to participate in a Middle Eastern peace conference, if one was convened. The Popular Front led the opposition against the Provisional Solution (a role it would continue to hold).

The debate in the spring and summer was intense. Arguing for support was the majority of Fateh and the Democratic Front. Both the Democratic Front and the Communists (who joined the PLO only in the mid-1980s) have always been more open to having a dialogue or negotiating with the Israelis than their fellow leftists in the Popular Front. The Popular Front, the Popular Front-General Command, and the Arab Liberation Front were the main groups of the Rejectionist Front, as they were called.

Inside the Women's Union, Fateh's Abu Khadra led the pro group with the argument that the international and regional power balance had changed in favor of Israel after its rapprochement with Egypt. Popular Front's Khaled led the opposition, arguing that this was a drastic departure from the PLO Charter and that armed struggle was the only chip left in the hands of the Palestinians to use against Israel.

In August, Arafat had gone straight from a trip to Moscow to the Lebanese summer resort of Sauq al-Gharb, where the Women's Union was holding its meeting at the Martyrs' Children's School. The leadership and everyone else expected the delegates to represent their own factions and vote the party line. Arafat, however, was concerned because his own Fateh caucus and the independents were not all behind his new policy. In addition to the rejectionists, Fateh's Sayigh, Helou, and Um Lutuf—and also the Union's president independent Abdel Hadi—were opposed to the Provisional Solution.

A great deal of the discussions at Sauq al-Gharb were behind closed doors, and the internal dynamics of what occurred, Helou revealed, was a battle of wills over the course of the PLO among leading elements of Fateh, its dominant faction, in which Arafat and his supporters won. Helou emphasized that the cadres that were critical of the Provisional Solution were brought into conformity by being forced to recognize the increasing importance of the United States and other Western powers during the course of the Palestinian movement. She said:

> What is important is that there were hugh pressures because Abu Ammar (Arafat) and the political leadership of the PLO wanted to assure the Americans and others that they control the

political decision making; not just the organization but the mass base, the grassroots and the syndicates. So it was very important that supporting decisions be made by all congresses of the popular unions. They tried their best. There were nights we didn't sleep. The members of the congress would come and debate, especially Fateh's caucus. The congress was delayed two days and the delegates knew there are problems and the political leadership could not enforce a supportive decision immediately.

This quote also confirms that, by the early 1970s, the women's organization had become an important segment of the nationalist movement that Arafat found necessary to woo in order to solidify his leadership.

Arafat scored a qualified victory when the Women's Union passed a compromise resolution. The women supported the Provisional Solution but also included a qualification that supported all decisions of the National Council—which meant supporting the 1968 National Charter and the armed struggle. Both Khaled and Abdel Hadi, however, had remained opposed. The compromise was face-saving for Arafat and his followers, but it left him unhappy with the renegades within his own faction.

Over the years, Women's Union president Abdel Hadi continued to argue for adherence to the letter of the PLO Charter, especially to the goal of a secular, democratic state in all of Palestine. For example, in 1988, at the 19th Palestine National Council, she voted against the National Council resolution that removed PLO opposition to UN Security Council Resolution 242—which effectively recognized Israel. After "emphasizing the inadmissibility of the acquisition of territory by war and the need to work for a just and lasting peace," UN Security Council Resolution 242 also said, "every state in the area can live in security." At the same time, Abdel Hadi was always supportive of Arafat's leadership of the PLO.

The debate at the Second Congress of the Women's Union left a bitter aftertaste among the hardliners and centrists alike. There was a sense that the process of decision-making was less than truly democratic. It was an impression that resurfaced during subsequent debates over the political course of the PLO. The women's leadership felt that National Council deliberations were open and vibrant but that decisions were ultimately made behind closed doors by Arafat and others in the top leadership.

Shortly after the Second Congress, Arafat temporarily "froze" the Women's Union, which meant he withheld Fateh's funding support; his supporters also boycotted secretariat meetings. In particular, Arafat was upset with Sayigh, who exhibited an independent streak, and there was talk of replacing her with a more disciplined cadre like Helou; she, however, was not interested. It was also a personal matter for Arafat because he and Sayigh had known each other for a long time and were from the same hometown, Gaza. In the tradition of old-style politics to which Arafat and his faction subscribed, Sayigh should have backed him up. "It was all related," said one observer. "What is important is that he froze the union for this reason: because he wanted the union to be in conformity with the political agenda."

Arafat's reprimand of the Women's Union lasted for six months, during which time the Sayigh-led secretariat supported its activities from funds from other resistance groups and from the Iraqi, Algerian, and Libyan women's unions. The secretariat itself maintained a fairly active travel schedule, sending delegations to meetings of the Cuban Women's Union in Havana and the Arab Women's Union in Baghdad. Delegates also traveled to Moscow, where they attended the preparatory meeting for the International Democratic Union, which subsequently admitted them to its ranks at its next conference in East Berlin.

The international activities proved to be a great asset to the image of the secretariat, enhancing its role as being representative of the Palestinian women. International work was mandated in the Women's Union Charter, Article 1, Section 9, which stated the union shall "establish and develop relations with Arab and friendly organizations and liberation movements in the world." But the trips during the Lebanese period took on added urgency because they occurred during the PLO's thrust toward international recognition and financial support.

The twelve months following the Women's Union Second Congress were particularly eventful. In October 1974, at the Rabat Arab Summit, the Arab countries voted unanimously to acknowledge the PLO as the "sole legitimate representative of the Palestinian People." A month later, Arafat addressed the UN General Assembly, raising the olive branch of peace to Israel if it would agree to a secular democratic state to be home to Israelis and Palestinians alike. The PLO secured an observer status at the United Nations, aided by a sympathetic Third-World and socialist majority at the UN General Assembly. And in November 1975, the UN General Assembly passed a resolution denouncing Zionism as a form of racial discrimination, which was repealed in 1992. The PLO's international campaign paid off with increased aid from the Arab oil-producing countries and eventual recognition by some ninety states.

It was in the midst of all this international hustle that the PLO women travelled to Mexico to attend the women's conference in 1975.

IV.

In July 1975, Abdel Hadi, Helou, and two other women travelled to Mexico City to represent the PLO at the first of three UN-sponsored Women's Decade conferences; the other two conferences were in Copenhagen in 1980 and Nairobi in 1985. The women were also advised by PLO Political Department diplomats: observer at the UN Zuhdi al-Tarazi, and Issam Kamel, who was stationed in Europe (advisors were also present at the other two conferences). One-third of the thirty-four leaders had attended one or more of these events, but several, those mainly from the Occupied Territories, could not attend because of the Israeli government's ban on their travel.

The Women's Decade conferences proved to be a great opportunity to take the message of the plight of the Palestinian people to the world. Helou, who was head of the union's external relations committee, attended all the conferences. She said:

> It was good to be able to put your struggle—and this is women's—as part of the struggle of other women. And for many in the feminist movement to show them that it is fruitless to think that you can separate your issues from the issues of your society and still talk about women.

The Mexico City meeting was especially successful because the Palestinians and their Arab allies got passed a resolution condemning Zionism as a form of racism. It was the testing ground for the anti-Zionism resolution, passed a few months later by the UN General Assembly.

How did they lobby? I asked PLO delegation chair Abdel Hadi. She said, "We divided the delegations like the Maghreb (North African countries) took those who [spoke] French, others took those who spoke English." She said the non-aligned, Muslim, and socialist European countries did not need to be lobbied much because they were supportive. She said:

> The secret of the success returns to the unity of the Arab women. There wasn't Camp David. There wasn't the Sinai Agreement (referring to the Egyptian-Israeli Peace Treaty of 1979). In 1975 we were united, Palestinians and Arabs, and we created miracles.

The Mexico City conference was the only one of the Women's Decade meetings where Arabs were so unified; this was symbolically displayed when they walked out en masse as head of the Israeli delegation, Mrs. Rabin, wife of the Prime Minister Yitzhak Rabin, began her speech. The day before, the Finnish president of the conference had tried to prevent the walkout. She asked the Palestinian delegation to cancel the floor demonstration, arguing that the conference should maintain an image of constructiveness and effectiveness. She wanted no trouble, especially since this was the first women's conference of such global magnitude.

Abdel Hadi's response was this:

> I told Mrs. Sipila (president of the conference) we are not protest-ing against the speech of Mrs. Rabin. We are protesting against the Zionist existence in Palestine and the ill-treatment of our people in Palestine. That is why we are going to walk out. It is not something personal against Mrs. Rabin or against the United Nations.

Sayigh and Helou led the Palestinian delegation to the 1980 confer-ence at Copenhagen, and were able to ward off any challenge to repeal the "Zionism is racism" resolution. Abdel Hadi was present for a couple of panels but could not stay because of illness; additionally, the conference was held during the Muslim holy month of Ramadan, and she wanted to be considerate and be with her husband at that time. At Nairobi, however, the fight with the United States proved more fierce, reflecting the changing global political environment of the mid-1980s. By that time, U.S. policy was to counter at every turn the UN resolution equating Zionism with racism.

Aside from women's conferences, Palestinian women were conspicu-ously absent from PLO international missions. Only on rare occasions were women (usually from Fateh) invited to join. Abu Khadra, for exam-ple, was in the delegation that travelled with Arafat to the UN General Assembly meeting. Helou said she did some early travelling with the men. She mentioned two trips, in 1969 with a delegation of men to India—"two younger men and myself," she said—and another in 1971, to the United States. "Afterwards, for a while, women stopped travelling," she said.

Why? I asked. "Part of it is *afawiya* (roughly translated as unintended) and part, perhaps, is that before there were so few (women)—so it was not an issue." Generally, Helou concluded, "They didn't think about it."

Abu Ali agreed with this assessment and said she herself often protested to the men in charge. She would say:

> Your delegation has about fifteen to sixteen persons. Why didn't you think to include one of us? You will go and find out that the delegations from the other movements or the delegations from the states that are coming no doubt they will include women. And also we share with you the political work, the *tanzim* (cadre)

work, the intellectual work. When there is decision making we are not [included].

The men's answer, she said, would be something like this: "No problem. 'There is no difference.' 'We didn't think.'" Then and now Abu Ali remains unconvinced and disheartened by such a response: "Sometimes they remember and sometimes they forget. If they forget with one delegation, they will remember with the next one. Then they will forget again," she said.

V.

With elections behind them, the leadership had to deal with the fundamental question of their tenure. The Lebanese period witnessed the longest, freest access of leaders to the Palestinian community in the diaspora, opening great opportunities for women's participation. The question was: how were they going to mobilize women for the Revolution?[5]

The second-generation leaders were schooled in the idealism of Nasser's era, which created an appetite for mass politics, and they were posed to challenge the restrictive social mores that discouraged women from participating. In the words of Helou:

> For most of us—our [leftist] current from other factions and some in Fateh, women's liberation or feminism was part of political and national liberation. We have to give special attention to the woman because of her situation, and we cannot say [there is] no problem and we are all equal.

However, the lessons from the Jordanian period warned that strategies of women's mobilization must be realistic and practical. In 1974, the Women's Union floated the slogans "land before honor" (*al-ard qable al-'ird*), "a vocational center in every camp," and "a kindergarten in every camp." Regardless of the faction or ideological orientation, these were goals on which all could agree. They were also a continuation of the centrist approach of the first generation, indeed, its basic mobilizational strategy. Jihan Helou said that meant addressing the families' basic needs:

> It wasn't enough to tell them, 'come let us do something for the struggle,' because they used to say, 'We are ready.' Whenever there was a crisis or real fighting they were in the front. They loved Palestine like we loved it and more. They were not ready for a systematic commitment in the struggle. . . . So talking or giving lectures became useless sometimes. So you had to do something which really touched their immediate interest, to feel

that through the union they can gain something that will help them face life.

To the leftists like Helou, practicality was a fundamental lesson of their leadership training:

> Maybe some people used to say this [our approach] was tradi-tional. But it was easy to do and not expensive. After all, we are not on our land and our means are limited. So we couldn't do any more than was possible. Sometimes, by training them, they could work either at home or in some of the small factories of the Revolution like Samed (PLO's economic arm). And at the same time we knew that economic and social problems cannot be solved except by liberating Palestine. You cannot solve your problems regardless [of circumstances]. But you can make changes and some advancement in their position. We never had illusions.

Local organizers who came out of the refugee camps knew this very well. Second-generation Maryam al-Atrash (a Fateh member of the secre-tariat since 1985) grew up in the Ein Hilwi camp in Lebanon and her fam-ily later on moved to the Yarmuk camp in Syria. Her political strategy drew on years of organizing at Yarmuk which, as all other camps, was a very conservative community. She explained that, because "our society is strict," one must:

> Establish a relationship with the family—and the father before the mother—so that we can bring out the young women. In the end, to reach the woman, you needed to feel her needs, evaluate her work, her life, her world, the relationship with her husband and children, the neighbors, her view of the school, how she will deal with her children, the teacher. Gather from people what their needs are and you take the common denominators.

Social traditions were particularly resistant to the secularism of the Marxist-Leninist Popular and Democratic fronts—both small in numbers with tightly knit cadre organizations. The two fronts exhibited a great deal of egalitarianism early on but, in the face of the prevailing conser-vatism of the Palestinian society in the camps, they made a hasty retreat. Their call for women's liberation remained mainly theoretical, arguing that the women's situation was a secondary oppression to both class and national oppression.

The Democratic Front, however, was known for being receptive to having women in leadership roles in its organization. Its women were known to be strong and independent, said one observer. The women of the Democratic Front were the first to sponsor a non-cadre women's organization in 1978, which emphasized the autonomy of women's decision-making (this is the idea that underscored the Women's Committees' Movement in the Occupied Territories).

Second-generation Muhammad was the leading Democratic Front woman in the Lebanese period. She explained:

> This was a serious development in methods of working in the women's sphere meaning, consecrating democracy inside the ranks. Getting her (the woman) used to the idea that there is no one in charge of her; she chooses those in charge.

This was necessary, said third-generation Abla Abu Elbi, who works for the Democratic Front in Jordan. "If we want to serve them, in fact, and if we want to be true leaders to the people in the future," she said, "we cannot isolate ourselves from them, or continue to talk in theories. I mean, there is no choice."

By 1975, however, the events in Lebanon became a constant reminder that strategies about building the female base of the Palestinian Revolution had to take second place to the reality of the war that prevailed. No refugee camp escaped the violence that halted not only literacy classes and crafts workshops at the women's centers but halted all thinking about new projects—as relief work took center stage. When the women's centers were hit, Abu Ali recalled, all the projects had to stop as women stayed home or in bomb shelters with their children. Much of the women's leadership energy was from that time on poured into humanitarian aid: it converted houses into hospitals; formed popular committees to visit the wounded and families of martyrs; arranged to feed the fighters; built shelters; and organized first aid training workshops with the help of the Palestinian Red Crescent.

The prize project of the Women's Union was Dar al-Sumud (house of steadfastness), an orphanage founded in 1976 for Tal el-Za'tar refugee camp children. Tal el-Za'tar was located in Christian East Beirut, but it fell after a nine-month siege by rightist forces. The other refugee camps in East Beirut were also destroyed and the residents evacuated to West Beirut (the predominantly Muslim section where Palestinian headquarters were located). The orphanage was later housed in a multi-story building at Bir Hassan near Beirut; it was there that the Women's Union tried to recreate a semblance of family, by organizing the children into groups of four or five, parented by adults. After their departure from Lebanon, the orphans were divided between facilities in Damascus and Tunis, neither remaining in the charge of the union.

Crisis situations were a grounding experience for the women's leadership, bringing a greater appreciation of the women in the camps. Third-generation Vera Naufal was deeply impressed by the strength of the women in the camps, as was earlier felt by second-generation Um Nasser in Jordan and Jehan Helou, who noted it after witnessing the 1969 camp uprising in Lebanon. Naufal said:

> The Palestinian woman carries all the burden. There are periods when men disappear, get jailed, killed, and the Palestinian woman is up to the challenge. I mean the traditional woman. She does everything in the house and for the children. She gets pregnant, gives birth, she builds houses and defends the camp, and goes to the first demonstration that goes out of the camp.

Observing the lives of these women during war also brought about a deeper understanding of how the larger political context affected the opportunities of liberation for women. Succinctly put by Naufal, "When water is cut off the camp that is a woman's issue."

Those members of the women's leadership who participated directly in the emergency work found they learned valued leadership skills they could not have acquired otherwise. For Abu Ali, this was an unexpected reward of participating in the Resistance, compensating for what she missed by abandoning her original life goal of graduate education and professional life:

> It was required of me and the *munadilat* (strugglers) who are with me in charge of an area under siege or in a war situation—we were expected—to clean an area. It was expected of us to provide vaccinations in an area, or organize the women to attend to hygiene and carry out economic activities at that time: kneading and baking bread and cooking. I mean, one gains familiarity with all details of life. A person acquires ability. . . . One acquires a complete and very rich experience. That is why I don't feel the loss.

Even as they were subjected to the vagaries of the civil war, Abu Ali and her colleagues at the Women's Union finally managed—mainly during the period 1975–1978—to build the popular base of their organization.

VI.

By the late '70s, the secretariat of the Women's Union presided over the greatest expansion in the history of its organization, some 25,000 members. The vast majority of members were from its flagship, the Lebanese branch, which meant the union was able to reach roughly 16 percent of the female adult refugees there.[6]

The structure of Lebanon's branch was complete with local commit- tees (south, north, Beirut area and so on) and a central executive. In 1978, open elections for the branch leadership were held; it was the only time in the history of the Union that free elections were possible—and on such a grand scale. The impartiality of the process was guaranteed by rules set by the PLO Department of Mass Organizations and by monitors from all the factions. It was a proud moment for Lebanese branch president Shadia Helou:

> The competition was great and honest so that no faction was able to stab the fairness of the elections because, in fact, everybody was watchful and participating and were present at the ballot box. I tell you there was a complete organizational structure. It was a great accomplishment in fact.

The secretariat also felt rewarded by the membership expansion in Lebanon but, at the same time, its hold on the Lebanese branch was always rather slippery. In part, this was due to the flexibility the branches enjoyed in devising their own strategies of attracting women. This was necessary because of the different parameters host countries set for Palestinian activism. Also, funding was not controlled by the secretariat but came from the central funds of the PLO and from the branches, in the form of membership fees, donations, and money from crafts bazaars.

The relationship of the secretariat with the Lebanese branch was made more difficult by the presence of the union headquarters in Beirut. Personal competition was partly responsible, with Sayigh arriving from Jordan needing to coexist with the Lebanese-based Fateh women's leader- ship, led by the Helou sisters. Ironically, the women's leadership faced a similar problem vis-a-vis the male leadership arriving from Jordan. Jihan Helou witnessed the transition of power from the local to the national leadership. "Maybe in 1969," she said, "we made more decisions but we were underground and limited. Then, later on, because we were in the same place as the leadership, our decisions were not that helpful."

There was also the jurisdictional issue with the secretariat wanting the branch to follow its own representation arrangement, making sure branch committees had representatives from the various factions. Fateh always stood for a united front, insisting that all currents in the movement be represented in the PLO's policy-making bodies. The problem was that, while its own female cadre was channeled to work in the Women's Union, the other factions carried on a more robust organizing effort for their own women's organizations. From the perspective of branch president Shadia

Helou, making sure all the factions were always represented in the leadership of the Lebanese branch was artificial, and not reflective of the political balance in the camps, which favored Fateh.

Indeed, the reality on the ground was that the women in the different factions, including Fateh, poured their energies into their separate political activities. Abu Ali said the dominant paradigm in the women's sphere was this:

> What happens is that every faction will get its women [membership] together into a women's organization or office that follows the affairs of women. If there is an important question, the office follows up on it with the faction or, in the case of the General Union of Palestinian Women, with the PLO [Executive Committee]. If we feel they are overlooking the question of the women, we remind them of it. If we feel there is a problem facing women, we try to help solve it. If we feel we need to work on a problem, we request funds. Like that.

The only times women in the different factions cooperated were when a large crowd was needed for a demonstration or to celebrate certain occasions such as the International Women's Day on March 8, or Land Day on March 30. Shadia Helou, who was president of the Lebanese branch for much of the 1970s, explained:

> We would have a sit-in at the Red Cross or a sit-in at the United Nations building, or a memorandum that needed to be signed. Who comes? The union's public. Who are the union's public? They are the tanzimat (plural for tanzim or cadre organization) that have joined under its wing.

In the end, factional women's organizations were a mixed blessing in the development of the Palestinian women's leadership. On the one hand, they widened the pool of women who could acquire political skills and leadership opportunities. But they also acted to entrench the idea of a separate women's sphere—giving a window of escape for the male leadership so it would not have to face women's social constraints.

This is something Um Jihad had tried to avoid—not having women and men together in the same cadre organization in Fateh. And she was able to develop her own power base in the male-dominated cadre organization through her leadership of the Families of the Martyrs foundation and because of her marriage to Abu Jihad. Everyone knew that working in the main arena—the cadre organizations, the social welfare institutions, the revolutionary media and so on—was acknowledged more as political work. In the words of Shadia Helou, "Frankly, from the beginning of the

movement, I wasn't that encouraged to work in the women's framework. I like the political work." Shadia Helou also thought women's work was very difficult: "It is not an easy matter because the woman remains the most backward of the sectors in the society." Most in the women's leadership, however, including the Helou sisters, tried to straddle both spheres, which was frustrating at best.

VII.

In 1978, the Palestinian women's leadership found itself entangled in another political controversy brought about by the Camp David agreement, which was signed in September of that year, and the peace treaty. which concluded in March 1979. The question centered on the Arab Women's Union, an umbrella organization comprised of government-sponsored Arab women's unions.

The women's leadership from Syria, Libya, the PLO and others that represented governments opposed to the Israeli-Egyptian rapprochement wanted to convene a meeting to condemn Camp David. The president of the Union, however, Egyptian Suhair Qalamawi, refused to convene the meeting. The opposition followed with a meeting in Algeria. It decided to hold an Arab women's conference anyway, and elected PLO Women's Union president Abdel Hadi to lead the preparatory committee. Abdel Hadi seemed headed to replace Qalamawi as leader of the competing Arab Women's Union.

The prevailing opinion in the opposition block was that Palestine was a common denominator on which all countries (especially rivals Syria, Libya, and Iraq) could agree. But then Arafat stepped in and convinced Abdel Hadi not to accept the nomination for president. One participant explained what happened:

> So in the beginning the political leadership, specifically Abu Ammar (Arafat), was not very enthusiastic for this union. It seemed he felt that the Arabs after Camp David, the Gulf states, al-Maghreb (North Africa) and even Iraq until 1978, were not very enthusiastic to condemn Camp David. So he wanted the union not to succeed. And then Iraq (joined the opposition to Camp David). There was a conference in Syria in 1981 and what was expected was that Issam (Abdel Hadi) would be the president but she—after the pressure—didn't want to enter into a conflict (with Arafat).

Abdel Hadi was subsequently chosen honorary president; a Syrian, Hamida Ali Manna, was elected president; and the new union's headquarters were temporarily moved to Libya (and later to Syria). Shortly after, Iraq joined the opposition against Camp David, and formed its second competing union, headquartered in Baghdad. Officially, in the Syrian-Iraqi competition, the Palestinian women's leadership stayed neutral and urged Arab unity, which was Arafat's position. In reality, the PLO's Women's Union secretariat was divided on this issue, with some of the leftists like Helou and Muhammad favoring the Syrian-based union and centrists like Um Nasser and Um Sabri siding with Iraq.

By the late '70s, it was apparent that the women's leadership could claim impressive achievement in gaining international visibility and in building the Women's Union. However, in the area of social welfare, in which it played a pioneering role, its contributions were dwarfed by other PLO organizations, as well as private societies. The Women's Union was now a recognized sector of the mobilizational framework of the PLO, but its share in the service-providing aspect of nation-building was small.

VIII.

The Women's Union was part of the Palestinian movement's extensive outreach in Lebanon (and to some extent in Syria), reaching every neighborhood and almost every family in the camps, through employment in PLO offices, Samed's mushrooming industries, the Families of the Martyrs foundation, and the Palestine Red Crescent Society's clinics and hospitals. Resistance factions, other than Fateh, and the charitable societies, such as the Palestine Aid Society, formed in 1977, carried out dozens of parallel projects in the camps as well.[7] The Women's Union's share in the Palestinian social welfare activities in Lebanon was modest, topping off at one kindergarten per camp and even fewer vocational centers. It also operated a few kindergartens in some of the other branches and, the wealthier ones, like Kuwait's, provided student scholarships. Overall, PLO institutions grew rapidly to meet the needs of the population from the mayhem of the Lebanese civil war, but also grew as an outcome of the expansion of PLO resources due to the influx of funds from the Gulf area. One observer said that large donations from Saudi Arabia and other conservative Arab regimes (and from salary withholdings of Palestinian employees in these countries) poured in around 1979.

The institutionalization of the Palestinian revolution was completed sometime around 1979, when the PLO leadership took charge of all funding to the mass organizations. From then on, funding requests were made to the PLO's finance department, the Palestine National Fund. In the case of the Women's Union, certain expenses like office rental and salaries for kindergarten teachers were placed as line items in the PLO budget; any other major expense had to be requested as needed. In addition, funds for training teachers and teaching aids were occasionally secured from United Nations and European development agencies and non-governmental organizations.

Unfortunately, the more institutionalized the Palestinian National Movement became, the more the women's leadership found it was presiding over a narrower scope of the mobilization, and the more it became removed from the women it led. One observer said, "From the day that the different unions [mass organizations] started to get a budget, they began to be spoiled because it became easy. . . . They didn't need to struggle to achieve." Institutionalization meant loss of autonomy, said another critic:

> The tie of the popular unions with the official position of the PLO, and not being permitted independent action and decision-making, has meant that for a long time the Women's Union has stopped being a popular union. Since it had stopped taking initiative and relies on the decisions of the leadership, it has become a union for the authorities.

At the end of the Lebanese period, the women's leadership could agree on three critical and related concerns. After a decade of mobilization, social constraints on women were paramount in preventing women's full participation in the Palestinian movement. It was true that a great deal was accomplished and many female cadres came from the camps. But the reality of the women's situation was that most recruits were young and many stopped being active after marriage. Also, when a female cadre married, she had a distinct disadvantage; sometimes even when her husband was a comrade, said Abu Khadra:

> There were many young women and men at that time who married each other. I mean, he was cadre and she was cadre. Maybe she was in a leading role as a cadre higher than him. But with her pregnancy and giving birth, he got more developed and freer. And he went out while she was tied to the family, house, and children.

Women in the camps had tremendous potential—something the civil war starkly revealed—but it was rarely realized in the long term.

The second point of consensus was that below the top leadership, sexism was rampant. This is illustrated by three women in the secretariat.

A Fateh member said:

> The leadership of the PLO did not have a serious approach toward developing the situation of the Palestinian woman

because of the prevailing reactionary mentality and norms that govern our society, and inside the framework of the organization. And whatever positiveness there is, it is only for publicity. That is why every initiative [to the leadership] from the union on this matter used to be met with rejection.

A Democratic Front member said:

On the political side, the man would be the picture of progress and liberation, etc, and, on the social side, he would wear his father's qumbaz (traditional turkish-style male dress). . . . Yes I will tell you, in our Arab and Palestinian society especially it is not easy for the woman to go out of the house all the time. . . . Not all the companions in the Front permit their wives and daughters to participate in this path or this tanzim. In fact we had difficulty in convincing them. But the long struggle has paid off and change has occurred.

And an Arab Liberation Front member said:

Men dominate the Palestinian woman even in her own framework. . . . The perception of the leadership and the perception of the man in the tanzim has not changed regarding the role of the woman, her capabilities and her rights; that is, he still doubts her capabilities. Even if she excelled, exhibiting great capabilities, he is jealous of her and won't permit her [to lead]. In such a case, he tries to reduce her role and destroy her.

The prevailing view among the leftists in the secretariat was that some kind of political training was needed for both female and male cadres. Abu Ali elaborated this need in her 1975 book about the status of women in the Palestinian movement. She called for a programmatic change that would involve new slogans, initiatives, educational programs, research, and structures of support.[8] Such an ambitious approach, however, required active commitment by the leaders of the factions—both male and female—commitment that did not materialize.

The centrists, led by Abdel Hadi and Abu Khadra, kept their conviction that the national question must consume all of their political energies. Issues like multiple marriages, reproductive freedom, and spousal abuse were not seriously discussed but were set aside because of "other important things" or because it was "not the right time."

The overwhelming reality during the Lebanese period was that persistent crises paralyzed any effort to construct an effective agenda for social change among the Palestinian refugees. This was evident to Jihan Helou, who made a last ditch effort (before the 1982 Israeli invasion and her exit from the leadership) to place on the agenda of the National Council in 1981 the question of the social problems of women—and she was rebuffed. The session held in Damascus was mired in dealing with the war in Lebanon, which had moved into higher gear. There were intense artillery battles and Israeli air raids on the Biqa' Valley and in the south and, on July 17, the Israeli airforce bombed Fateh and Democratic Front's headquarters in Fakahani. "There is always an external problem in the Palestinian arena," Abu Ali summed it up, "and that is why our issue becomes secondary or comes third or fourth even."

The last point of consensus among the women's leadership was that all its efforts did not pay off with a larger role in decision making. If anything, institution-building resulted in decisions moving upward to the male leadership. To Abu Khadra, it was always the case that "planning is with the men of the *tanzim*, communication of information and mobilization with the women." The women's leadership, however, was posed for gains for women in the movement, such as more seats in the National Council. After what it viewed as a decade of contributions, the women's leadership felt it had proven itself.

The secretariat had one last chance to bring to attention these issues in 1981, when it held a symposium on the situation of Palestinian women in the movement. The PLO leaders all came—Fateh's Yasser Arafat, Popular Front's George Habash, Democratic Front's Nayef Hawatmeh and the rest. One speaker after the other presented research papers that confirmed what all had known—that there were enormous social and economic obstacles in the path of women's participation in the movement.

Muhammad, who was head of the cultural committee in charge of the program, thought the symposium actually brought about a twelve-seat addition (from about four or five) to the women's block in the National Council. Actually, this increase was also part of the PLO leadership's drive to expand the representation of all mass organizations (that eventually gained them one-third of the seats). The increase in the number of women, however, resulted in second generation comprising the majority of women in the Council.

IX.

The Lebanese period ended in the summer of 1982. Israel invaded Lebanon on June 6 and drove straight north to Beirut. West Beirut was heavily bombarded during a nine-week siege that ended with the PLO's withdrawal. All the leading women who were in Beirut had to be evacuated, along with the various Palestinian militias. In August, a multinational United Nations force landed in Beirut to supervise the withdrawal of the PLO forces. The Palestinian militias left primarily by ship, to Cyprus and Greece, and were then distributed among several friendly Arab countries. Other PLO workers, including most of the women, travelled via land to Damascus. (Sayigh kept a personal diary of the siege of Beirut and the PLO exit, which she published in 1988.[9]) And, the PLO found a new home in Tunis.

Um Nasser left with the militias to Greece and from there to Tunis. She told the story of how she first tried to leave aboard a Red Cross ship called Flora, disguised as a nurse. A Red Cross official had recognized her and said, "There is no one who doesn't know Um Nasser because she is at brother Abu Ammar's office." So she had to be disguised as a wounded militia. Um Nasser said, "I had to put on a leg cast and I went; in fact, I was carried. Of course, that was a bit embarrassing because I had to wear a hospital gown."

Others, like Mai Sayigh and Jehan Helou, were able to stay on a while longer before traveling to Damascus, leaving the relief work in the hands of volunteers on the ground. Reports filtered in from Israeli-occupied southern Lebanon, telling how local women from the camps carried on with relief work, including instances where women were killed while carrying food to the fighters and to children and families in the camps.

The camps in West Beirut were particularly vulnerable, in that they were near the hub of the Palestinian Resistance at Fakahani. In September, hundreds of residents in the Sabra and Chatilla camps were massacred by the Lebanese rightist militias while under the protection of the Israeli army. After, women played the key role of communicating with the multi-national forces who came to protect the camps. (One woman said they made lists of names of those who were arrested and kidnapped from the camps and delivered them to the media so that, "the light on what happened to the Palestinians is not eclipsed.")

With the men shipped out, in hiding, or killed, the women held the community together, guiding the relief work of the Red Cross and the various European teams from Italy, Norway, Austria, and from Lebanese and Palestinian wealthy families. The PLO left funds which, according to Sayigh, included three-month advance salaries to all workers in PLO institutions.[10] The funds were left mainly in care of the *shabab*. Why the young men? I asked. It was the custom—the funds were simply given to PLO representatives who were men. Jihan Helou was again critical:

> There should have been the thinking that in difficult times, it is the women who take the leadership. Of course, we are proud of this role. It is natural that the woman would take charge. We didn't take it because it was planned but because the circumstances made it imperative and we took the initiative and at the

same time there was great courage because some of the women were well known and some were arrested.

In 1983, in the aftermath of the Israeli withdrawal, Syrian troops returned and entered most of the Palestinian refugee camps, taking charge of the Women's Union centers and kindergartens. UNRWA maintained its educational and relief services—as it did throughout the period of PLO control of the camps. Also active in relief were the private women's groups such as the Palestine Aid Society, operated by women associated with the Democratic Front.

Also in that year a visitor to a camp in Beirut noticed increased use of the Muslim veil, replacing the kaffiyeh, the Arab headcover that had become the symbol of the Palestinian Resistance. The Women's Union center at Chatilla was also repaired in 1983 and, on March 8, it celebrated the International Women's Day.

They had all been through war and exile before—Sayigh, Um Nasser, Abu Ali, Um Sabri and others in the second generation who came with the Resistance from Jordan. But the Beirut tragedy was more devastating because of the extended and senseless violence—because they had glimpses of success in nation-building among the refugee camps; because their revolution was institutionalized in Lebanon; and because they and the Revolution had aged. When they left Beirut, they knew the Middle East region was changing. It was a different world, one where slogans of anti-colonialism and anti-reactionaries no longer mattered; oil power and financial wealth did. The end of the Lebanese period was devastating because, on top of the grief, there was no paradigm for what they had experienced and they did not know what could come next.

Chapter 4

TUNIS
Decline of Mobilization in the Palestinian Diaspora

I.

Official records at the Women's Union headquarters in Tunis date back only to 1985; there are no minutes of the secretariat meetings for the period 1983–1985, and all the official documents in Lebanon were destroyed in the 1982 departure. What happened to the union? I asked former leader Sayigh, when I saw her in Amman in 1991. "It is empty," she said tersely, noting the naked truth that the era of mobilization for the Palestinians in the diaspora had ended.

The best the leadership could have hoped for after Lebanon was that the union was only in a state of limbo. Some thought it could have been revitalized by the infusion of new blood and a more aggressive women's agenda, but the odds were heavily stacked against any optimism. The loss of Lebanon had meant an immediate and permanent drop in membership—to roughly 5,000–10,000 from the height of 25,000. Most of the local organizers were out of action, killed during the last days of the violence, forced into exile or pulled into private life.

Some of the die-hard veterans from Lebanon's arena resurfaced in one of the other Union branches and started new branches in Cyprus and Tunis. Hundreds of Palestinian expatriates from Lebanon ended up there, along with most of the PLO offices. (In the early 90s, other efforts by the Women's Union secretariat to organize branches in Britain and the United States got off to a slow start mainly because of little interest in political mobilizing on the part of the Palestinian women there. Also, in the United States, Popular and Democratic fronts' women's groups had long had independent organizations, and therefore, were reluctant to submit to Fateh's leadership out of Tunis.) The situation of the women's leadership in the diaspora never improved, swept by the leadership crisis that plagued the PLO from the moment it departed Lebanon.

During the period 1983–1984, the PLO broke into three clusters, sending into political oblivion the two leaders of the Women's Union during the Lebanese period.[1] The casualties were Fateh's Mai Sayigh and Jehan Helou, who lost their seats in the secretariat when they joined the forces that were critical of Arafat.

Helou, who was one of Fateh's pioneers in Lebanon, sided with the National Alliance, which was in open rebellion against Arafat and backed by Syria. There were four factions in this block: Sa'iqa, the Popular Front-General Command, the Palestine Struggle Front, and rebels from Arafat's own faction, the Fateh-Provisional Command. The National Alliance presented three main grievances: (1) There was rampant corruption in the PLO bureaucracy; (2) Arafat was wrong to have agreed to leave Lebanon and its large Palestinian population; and (3) Arafat should not have sought rapprochement with Jordan and Egypt. Jordan was considered an enemy because of its war on the Resistance in 1970–1971, and Egypt was held in disfavor because of its peacemaking with Israel in 1979.

Sayigh, whose friendship with Arafat dated back to the Jordanian period and is from his hometown of Gaza, supported the Democratic Alliance, which opposed Arafat's centralized leadership. This block contained most of the major PLO groups: the Popular Front, the Democratic Front, the Palestine Liberation Front, and the Palestine Communist Party. These groups were critical of Arafat's personalized leadership, but were committed to the unity of the PLO and its independence from outside control, a commitment deeply shared with Arafat's Fateh. In a sense, the defiance of the Democratic Alliance was much more important to Arafat than the rebellion of the National Alliance, because the Democratic Alliance represented some of the most active Palestinian groups that had long histories of popular organizing and commando operations. In turn, Arafat kept the allegiance of the bulk of Fateh and also the Iraqi-sponsored Arab Liberation Front.

During the period 1986–1987, the internal struggle in the Palestinian National Movement was brought under control, and all the major groups returned under the PLO umbrella and Arafat's leadership. Several factors brought about the reunion, not the least of which was that Arafat had kept the loyalty of "the street," especially the critical refugee camps. He was also able to rely on the support of almost all the Arab countries—the exception being Syria.

The Palestinian rapprochement was also aided by having to cooperate closely during the period 1985–1987 in the so-called "war of the camps" in Lebanon and against the Iron Fist policy in the Occupied Territories. In Lebanon, PLO militias, that infiltrated back after the 1982 departure, engaged in defending several of the major refugee camps there, like Sabra, Chatilla, and Bourj Barajneh camps, against siege and shelling by the powerful Lebanese Shiite militia Amal. The Iron Fist policy, initiated in 1985 by then Israeli Defense Minister Yitzhak Rabin, aimed to put a halt to Palestinian nation-building, and targeted nascent worker's, women's, and other mobilizational organizations that were gaining strength.[2] The Occupied Territories were the new and final arena of confrontation between Israel and the PLO, and the PLO was preparing for the showdown with a vigorous institution-building drive centered in East Jerusalem, Ramallah, Nablus, and Gaza.

The PLO schism officially ended at the 18th session of the National Council held in 1987. The PLO reunion agreement was based on the so-called "minimum of understanding." This meant the parties agreed to disagree on strategies to regain the homeland, but were united in affirming the PLO as the unchallenged voice of the Palestinian liberation movement. All but the members of the National Alliance were represented—and joined the PLO for the first time the Palestine Communist Party.

Sayigh, who supported the Democratic Alliance, never returned to the Women's Union. However, her relationship with Arafat was mended and, for a short while, she was attached to his Tunis office as an advisor. In the early 1990s, Sayigh was living a more or less private life in Paris and in Amman, while keeping in close touch with her friends in the Fateh leadership.

Helou also remained in private life, studying for a Ph.D. and working for an Arab daily newspaper in London. Helou has since had only a rare foray into political life—for example, she presided over the first conference of the Women's Union branch in London in 1991 and during the elections of its first officers. Her participation in the British branch might bring her into better terms with the current women's leadership, but her involvement at this point is minimal.

Laila Khaled of the Popular Front was no longer in the secretariat, having left for university study in 1980. After the mid-1980s, however, both Khaled and Democratic Front's Nihaya Muhammad (who remained in the secretariat) held leadership posts as heads of their factions' respective women's organizations, headquartered in the large Yarmuk camp in Syria.[3] In Yarmuk, one still finds the familiar kindergartens, adult women literacy classes, health education, and sewing classes.

On the surface, political activity among the women of Yarmuk did not look much different than that of the Lebanese period. This was, however, a different time and place, when armed militias no longer walked the streets and where Palestinians were controlled by their host, the Syrian government. It was also the time when the women's leadership found it had become realistic about the pace of social change for women. The leftists, regardless of their faction, had travelled full circle from the late 1960s, returning to more non-threatening social services. This had always been the mainstay of women's political work and was sponsored by the factions, who paid the salaries of full-time cadres and the rentals of offices and women's centers. International development funding grants from European countries and private agencies and from UNICEF and UNESCO helped with women's projects at the local level, but mainly in the Occupied Territories.

The departure of Sayigh, Helou, and Khaled from the Women's Union secretariat signalled the end of an era in the history of the organization. In the late 1980s, political disagreements among the factions were no longer starkly mirrored in the Women's Union. The outcome of the schism within Fateh was that, for those women who remained with Arafat, the spirit of team loyalty would prevail. The agreement of "minimum of understanding" between the factions meant that the different cadre organizations, though still represented in the Women's Union, had gone their different ways. It was a confirmation of a long-prevailing belief that the Union was in reality a shell, and what was left of it was held by Fateh. To one cadre, it was as if "Mai and Jehan left with the union in their pocket."

II.

The headquarters of the Women's Union was in the Fifth Manzah of Tunis, a pristine modern section of embassies and middle-class homes. The spacious three-story building was far removed from any of the large communities of Palestinians. To some, this distance symbolized a retreat into fruitless passivity. "What are they doing in Tunis far away from the Palestinians?" asked one Fateh cadre who lived in Jordan, adding, "Ok, bring the headquarters to Jordan—at least close to the camps." The geography of Tunis, however, was an unmistakable reminder of the homeland, sharing the coastal planes of Israel, Lebanon stretches of greenery, the mild climate, and the blue Mediterranean.

Centrists, sworn in at the Women's Union's Fourth Congress in 1985, were at the helm. They were led by president Issam Abdel Hadi and general-secretary Salwa Abu Khadra, who replaced Sayigh as operational head. The daily operations of the headquarters were supervised by Um Nasser, who went there after retiring from Arafat's office in 1986. Members of the secretariat, however, remained dispersed among several Arab countries, but a large contingent was in Amman, where Abdel Hadi still resided.

After the PLO reunited in 1987, the women's leadership returned to a semblance of normalcy. The structure of the leadership was maintained by the previous formula of Fateh majority (nine of the fifteen seats), two from allied Democratic Front, and one each from the Palestine Communist Party and the Arab Liberation Front, and two independents including Abdel Hadi.[4]

The minutes of the Women's Union secretariat from May 1985 to February 1990 showed irregular but usual business: attendance of international meetings; communications with friendly international unions and other groups; press conferences about current development in the Palestinian movement; raising funds and marketing of Palestinian embroidery; and visiting wounded cadre (this time from the October 1985 Israeli attack on the PLO headquarters in Tunisia).

The Tunis centrists and Damascus leftists proved to be the diehards, survivors who stayed the course through the wars and internal struggles. Without freedom to mobilize in the refugee camps of the diaspora, the leaders also shared a loss of power. It was not just that their struggle to unify the energies of Palestinian women for national liberation had regressed. They had also arrived at a void, for they had come to realize that there was not much they could do among the diasporan Palestinian community.

The situation was different with the leadership's international activities, as they had to respond to the rumbles of the revolution in East-West relations. The change in the global political environment rendered traditional friendships with friendly regimes and movements insecure. The veterans in the women's leadership had seen the winds of change as early as the 12th National Council in 1974. Then, Arafat successfully argued for the Provisional Solution, which opened the PLO to a political compromise with Israel based on partition. That was Arafat's first attempt to bring about a political resolution of the Palestinian problem, and it was meant to bring along Western governments—especially the United States.

Some two decades later, the women's leadership witnessed firsthand the ascendence of the United States to world leadership on the Palestine question. The place was Nairobi, where the Palestinians arrived in the summer of 1985 to attend the last Women's Decade conference.

III.

The Palestinians arrived in Nairobi in the middle of two new crises: the War of the Camps in Lebanon and Yitzhak Rabin's Iron Fist policy in the Occupied Territories. Khadijeh Abu Ali led the Palestinian effort in the Forum, which was the unofficial conference of the non-governmental organizations. The Forum was a receptive arena of hundreds of panels, providing the Palestinians with vast opportunities to tell about the plight of the Palestinians in the Occupied Territories and in Lebanon. Their team, however, was small—about thirty women and a few male advisors—and their work was as exhausting as it was exhilarating. Abu Ali said they tried to attend as many workshops as their energies and resources could stretch, adding:

> One summarized the papers according to the topic. If it was about development, we talked about development. If it was about education, we talked about education. It was about abused women, we would say how we have that with the women whose homes were demolished or their husbands are in prison.

This time, the PLO team was aided by a few women from the West Bank who were able to get Israeli exit visas to attend, though none came from the top leadership in the Occupied Territories. Until the late 1980s, leading women from the territories were routinely declined permission to travel by the Israeli authorities; sometimes, they were also under house or town arrest or in prison under administrative detention orders. However, the West Bank contingent proved very valuable by providing much needed up-to-date information about the conditions of Palestinian women under Israeli occupation.

Former Women's Union official Jihan Helou had attended the two previous Women's Decade conferences, and she was at Nairobi—though not in the official Palestinian delegation. Women from both sides of the PLO schism agreed to set aside their factional conflicts and cooperate. Actually, at that time, the main PLO groups—the Popular and Democratic fronts, the Palestine Communist Party and Fateh—were already in negotiations that preceded their reconciliation of 1987.

Abu Ali said it was necessary to reach out to all the attending Palestinian women because of the opposition that the United States mounted against the Palestinians. She said:

> We took them aside. We told them there is an open battle against us as Palestinians and they don't know who is in the PLO and who is outside it. There is a problem for us as Palestinians and the attempt is to take the resolution from us.

The battle with the United States was waged at the official conference, where the PLO faced a determined opposition from the United States' delegation led by President Reagan's daughter, Maureen. The United States accused the Palestinians of attempting to derail the conference, and the Palestinian cause was portrayed as subsidiary. Gregory Newell, U.S. Assistant-Secretary of State for International Organizations Affairs was quoted as saying, "We think it unwise to isolate 1,000 Palestinian women as an issue and reject the concerns of 2.4 billion other women in the world."[5]

The United States mounted a successful effort to make sure that Zionism was not specifically branded as racism—as had happened at the 1975 Mexico City meeting. The final resolution referred specifically only to apartheid. Paragraph 95 of the Forward-Looking Strategies read:

> Other major obstacles to the implementation of goals and objectives set by the United Nations in the field of the advancement of women include imperialism, colonialism, neo-colonialism, expansionism, apartheid and all other forms of racism, exploitation, policies of force and all forms or manifestations of foreign occupation, domination and hegemony, and the growing gap between the levels of economic development of developed and developing countries.[6]

Abu Khadra headed the PLO's official delegation, which was seated because the PLO had an observer status at the United Nations—voted in by the Third World majority in the General Assembly in 1974. But now, Abu Khadra and her colleagues found they could no longer rely on their traditional allies. The Soviet Camp was in the process of rapprochement with the West, signalling a global dealignment that stretched to the farthest corners of the Third World. And the Arabs were far from unified because of the Israeli-Egyptian Peace Treaty that distanced Egypt, the Iran-Iraqi war (that had Syria standing in opposition to Iraq), and the 1983–1987 schism in the Palestinian camp.

The changing international environment was particularly shocking to Maryam al-Atrash, who was attending her first Women's Decade conference. Al-Atrash was a newcomer, having been elected to the Women's Union secretariat just a couple of months earlier at the Union's Fourth General Conference held in Tunis. She was unique among the leadership in that she was raised in a refugee camp, Ein el-Hilweh in Lebanon, and therefore had more intimate knowledge of the refugee camps' traditions and how to mobilize the women there. Al-Atrash was a daughter of Fateh with a long-term commitment to the faction, including a brother who was a militia commander and another who was killed. In 1968, she and her family had relocated to Yarmuk camp in Syria and, by the early 1980s, she had risen from an organizer in the Yarmuk camp to a position of leadership in the Women's Union branch in Syria. In 1985, she had to move again, this time to Tunis, because of the rift between Arafat and the Syrian government. International relations, however, were a new experience to her and, at Nairobi, she saw firsthand the power play between United States' officials and some of the Third World delegates. She said:

> On the official level it was something else. In fact, we felt a lot how money, capitalism, and economics dominated. It wasn't a question of conscience, reason, or right. I mean, states, for example, African states, were threatened with aid cut-off. I mean, I was sitting behind a head of one of the delegations—I must have looked maybe Spanish—I was sitting behind her to talk with her to vote on our side. One came and sat next to her and talked to her and threatened her right in front of me: "If you vote in favor of the Palestinian resolution, you will be finished." I mean, to this degree in the middle of the conference while we are sitting.

The new global environment challenged the women's leadership to expand its external relations toward the West. At the diplomatic level, the PLO was already positioned to do so through long-nourished relations with the European community (for example, it had an informal relationship with France dating back to 1975).[7] The international strategy of the women's leadership, however, was solely based on solidarity friendships with women's federations in Soviet block and Third World regimes and liberation movements. And these were rapidly dismantling. The Palestinian women's leadership learned in Nairobi that its international strategy must begin to accommodate the new reality of Western dominance, and it suggested reaching out to non-governmental women's organizations in Western Europe, the United States, and even Israel. It was a challenge for which the Women's Union was ill-prepared, with its experience developed primarily from interactions with official unions.[8]

Afterwards, what the PLO team most remembered about the Nairobi conference was its tireless effort to tell the Palestinian story. Participating in Nairobi was an important nationalist task, and the women's leadership felt it did a good job—as good as its resources and the global political environment permitted. Nairobi was also the last spectacle in which the women's leadership of the diaspora took center stage, for, after the Intifada, the 1987 uprising in the Occupied Territories, all attentions and resources of the Women's Union and the national movement turned there.

The end of the 1980s therefore capped two decades of women's contributions to the Palestinian movement in the diaspora. It was a good time to assess the inroads women made toward participation in the policy-making bodies of the PLO. The statistics in 1990, however, gave an ambiguous picture of advances, while the top remained an almost exclusive men's club.

IV.

The PLO factions are governed by general congresses that elect policy-making interim bodies (Fateh's Revolutionary Council and Democratic and Popular Fronts' Central Committees), above which is the top executive leadership (Fateh's Central Committee, and Democratic and Popular Fronts' Political Bureaus). The equivalents at the national level are the Palestine National Council, the Central Council, and the Executive Committee.

The factional congresses operate much like party general meetings, occasions for the local leadership and party loyalists to meet, discuss, and vote on the party platform. Perhaps the greatest challenge to these meetings was logistical, being able to get exit visas for all the delegates and finding a hospitable government to host them. It was especially a problem for the National Council, which required finding a host who was not hostile to any of the factions—after Lebanon, that generally meant Algeria. Factional congresses tended to meet infrequently, with decisions relegated to the smaller interim policy bodies and the top executive leadership.

Keeping records of membership in national liberation movements is bound to be fraught with guesswork, and the PLO was not an exception. The percentages given here for each faction came from that group's women's leadership. Among the three main PLO factions with long histories of mobilization, the Democratic Front fared the best, with females constituting 28 percent of the membership, 17 percent of the Central Committee, and 13 percent of the Political Bureau. The Popular Front followed, with women constituting 15 percent of its cadres, 5 percent of the Central Committee—but none in the Political Bureau. The Popular Front was also coming to grips with the problem of sexism in its ranks, installing at the start of 1990 a new cadre evaluation policy that included how the members treated women.

It is especially difficult to learn about women's membership in the PLO's largest group Fateh because it is a loosely organized faction. Fateh followed the traditional party model that relied more on local bosses and patronage. The faction's general congresses were the best places to observe the progress of women; the fifth of these congresses was held in Tunis in 1989. Women constituted 7 percent of the delegates of Fateh's

Fifth Congress (80 of a total of 1100 delegates), up only 2 percent from the Fourth Congress in 1980.

Fateh's Fifth Congress also elected six women (up from one) to the eighty-member Revolutionary Council (7.5 percent). The six women elected came from a field of eight nominations and, on the surface, electing three-quarters of the women nominated looked good. It was, however, neither an effect of a unified women's strategy nor a patent decline in sexism. In fact, while four of the winners were from the Women's Union secretariat, they had not run on a common women's slate. The women candidates "promoted themselves individually," said one of the delegates.

Maisoun Sha'ath, who was a delegate to Fateh's congress and a member of the Women's Union secretariat, voiced caution about the Revolutionary Council results. Sha'ath's credentials in the Palestinian movement were strong, being a second-generation Fateh cadre who belonged to a well-known nationalist family who backed Arafat. She is also the sister of Nabil Sha'ath, who sits in Fateh's Central Committee and is a key mover in the peace negotiations with Israel. Maisoun Sha'ath lives in Cairo and is a rarity in the secretariat, in that she is not a full-time politico but also works in a company her brother owns. Sha'ath thought the women's success was mainly due to the willingness of male delegates to accept more readily the women from competing Fateh groupings. Women were viewed as less threatening than the men, she said. The groupings inside Fateh's congress consisted of various militia units, geographic regions, and PLO administrative units that were initially founded by Fateh (Samed, the Families of the Martyrs foundation, etc.).

But Fateh's Fifth Congress also elected the first woman, Um Jihad, to its top Central Committee (the vote for her was 824, from the total of 1100 delegates). Some thought this advancement was to honor Um Jihad for her husband's martyrdom—he was killed by Israeli commandos the previous year. This no doubt was the impetus, but Um Jihad herself was very well-respected for her years of sacrifice and hard work, alongside Abu Jihad and at the helm of the Families of the Martyrs.

Fateh's Fifth Congress seemed to have left an ambiguous message about the status of women in its cadre organization. To some in the women's leadership, these were only symbolic gains; progress was simply not sufficient given women's many years of contributing to the national effort. This was the conclusion reached by Abu Khadra, one of the women advised at the 1968 Damascus meeting with Fateh leader Abu Lutuf that they must strive to prove themselves in the struggle. Now, though she has risen to membership in Fateh's Revolutionary Council, she believes that "the thinking [inside Fateh] is still traditional, even after twenty-five years, even when the woman has proven herself."

Shadia Helou, who was also a long-term Fateh member, agreed, but thought women should share in the blame. She said, "I am not only putting the burden on the man but also the woman—basically, the woman who is aware, the cadre. She is taking it easy about herself and her rights." Helou, who was former president of the Women's Union Lebanese branch, thought it was always difficult to mobilize women because of their social situation, but with the loss of Lebanon and the few resources available it has become nearly futile. After Lebanon, Helou left the women's arena for a writing job at the PLO headquarters in Tunis.

The problem of low female representation in the factional congresses was due mainly to resistance at the middle leadership ranks—the people who actually attend the party congresses. In Fateh, for example, delegates are usually the top three or so leaders from the various party groupings. And it is not just the problem of sexist attitudes in the ranks. These middle-level leadership roles had monetary rewards attached to them and therefore the competition could be fierce.

The consensus among the women's leadership was that the top leaders were appreciative of what the women contributed and were supportive of their advancement to leadership. PLO Ambassador to the Netherlands, Laila Shahid, said, "Arafat is very responsive to the women's question. He is, in particular, sensitive to women who have proven their courage and their strength." Shahid and Nuha Tadrus were appointed to the ambassadorial rank in 1989—the first-ever female PLO ambassadors. Arafat, explained one of the women, wanted to recognize the women in the Intifada but he also aimed to transform the image of the Palestinians to show that they are a progressive people.

In 1990, virtually everyone I met from the PLO said that there was fresh interest in women because of their participation in the Intifada. The late Ahmad Abdel Rahim (died in 1991), who was chairman of the Arab Liberation Front and head of the PLO's Department of Mass Organizations, said the Intifada showed an unequivocal advancement in women's participation. It was as though women in the West Bank and Gaza crossed a barrier and suddenly became visible and important.

The Declaration of Independence, passed at the 19th session of the National Council in 1988 in Algiers, retained flowery references to the traditional imagery of heroism, calling women "brave" and guardians of "sustenance and life," and keepers of "our people's perennial flame." But it also made a commitment to equality "between the woman and the man," along with equality regardless of color and religion. The 19th session also sent an external message to the international community, that the Palestinians agree to a two-state solution based on withdrawal from the 1967 Occupied Territories and negotiations.

Reports from several of the female delegates said there was a consensus about the principle of equality and that no lobbying was needed. In any case, in the National Council, the women fall into the tightly controlled voting blocks of the factions. Even women's gains in terms of representation reflect quota arrangements agreed upon by the factions and, since 1984, the women's quota has been stable at 9 percent. The number of women in its eighty-member interim Central Council was one, Abdel Hadi, until the 20th session in 1991, when it rose to five.

Since the Intifada, however, some from among the diasporan women's leadership were pondering about what their role might be in the upcoming stage of state formation. Their thinking reflected the reality that the spotlight was now on the Occupied Territories and the women's organizations there.

V.

In February, 1990, the Women's Union secretariat met in Tunis, and one of its agenda items was the multi-paged Palestinian Family Identity card (*daftar al-'aila*). The PLO economic institution Samed had recently offered the card to Palestinians for purchase. The card had no legal standing and was merely a symbolic gesture of Palestinian nationalism. Samed occasionally marketed, or freely distributed, such emblems crafted into flags, watches, jewelry, and embroidery. The multi-page card contained the usual personal information such as age, sex, profession, religion, and marital status.

The problem with the identity card, as the secretariat saw it, was the provision of religious affiliation and listing of up to four wives under marital status—the maximum that a Muslim man could marry at one time. The secretariat sent its objections in a brief memorandum that was hand-delivered to the office of the PLO Executive Committee. The memorandum expressed concern that the identity card negated the spirit of equality and pluralism of beliefs enshrined in the Palestinian Declaration of Independence proclaimed by the 19th National Council in 1988.

Criticism of the identity card had travelled to Tunis from several of the Women's Union branches. Views were also heard at the headquarters at a general meeting called by the secretariat to inform the Palestinian women's community in Tunis of its decision to protest the identity card. The expatriates meeting was attended by several dozen women, many of whom worked at the PLO offices. Views expressed at the meeting repeated the concerns of the leadership but there was also a call for caution. Some said this might not be the time to bring up women's issues; others said issues should only be brought up to the PLO leadership if the women were prepared to tackle them; and still others said a wider discussion about the future Palestinian personal status law should be initiated with both female and male cadres.

The Palestinian identity card died a quick death when the PLO Executive Committee promptly put a halt to its distribution. Informal conversations between members of the Executive Committee and the secretariat revealed that the decision to issue the card had not been previously discussed. Apparently, some did not know about it until the Women's Union memorandum, but Arafat, one of the women was told, had given his permission. In sum, the women's leadership received the familiar, ambiguous mix of annoyance expressed as "do we need this now" and support of the women's contention that the card was indeed an ill-considered idea.

Nevertheless, the brief identity card affair conveyed the message that the women were intent on being vigilant and did not intend to repeat the Algerian women's experience—those women who fought in the resistance against French colonialism but lost out after independence. But there was also a noticeable tentativeness in the PLO's women's community, which was long accustomed to the paternalism that permeated the organization. The secretariat was torn by the need to balance its roles as delegates and leaders. It was a dilemma familiar to all dutiful partisans, and it was the fundamental challenge facing the women at the outset of the 90s.

VI.

For five days, in September 1991, the PLO's parliament, the 468-seat Palestine National Council, sat in its 20th session in Algiers. The meeting was called by Arafat to vote on his proposal to support the Middle East Peace Conference that was to begin in Madrid at the end of October. The purpose of the National Council was to make such major decisions; the term used to describe this role is *al-qarar al-filastini* (the Palestinian decision or consensus).

Altogether, forty-three women attended the 20th session; forty-one from the Women's Union (including two unknowns added by the PLO leadership to increase the North American delegation) and one each from the General Union of Palestinian Teachers and General Union of Palestinian Lawyers. During my 1990–1991 tour of the Middle East, I interviewed eighteen of these women.

The Women's Union representatives are the largest group (27 percent) among the PLO mass organizations—the category in the National Council that represents women, student, professional, and worker unions and syndicates. The mass organizations category is one of four roughly equal groupings represented in the National Council. The other three are Palestinian communities, independents (sometimes called notables), and the political-military resistance organizations of the different factions. The last grouping includes the Palestine Liberation Army whose units are housed alongside the militaries of Syria, Egypt, and Jordan. (The Palestinian police sent to Jericho and the Gaza Strip came in part from the Palestinian army in Egypt and Jordan.)

Theoretically, women could be elected from any of the four components but, in reality, society leaders such as Samira Ghazaleh and those in the militias such as Bernawi were placed on the Women's Union list. In the end, the strength of the women's representation was based on a fairly stable quota, long negotiated by the factions.

The heart of the women's delegation at the 20th session was the Women's Union's fifteen-member secretariat and leading members of its forty-six-seat administrative council. Conspicuous among the women were the revolution's luminaries: head of the Families of the Martyrs foundation, Um Jihad; Wedad Abdel Rahim, wife of leader of the Arab Liberation Front (who died of a heart attack in 1991); and former commandos Fateh's Bernawi, Popular Front's Khaled, and Democratic Front's Odeh, who sat in her party's Political Bureau. The entire distribution of seats in the National Council, however, was carefully balanced to maintain the previous distribution of factions. Abla Abu Elbi, who, along with Nihaya Muhammad, represented the Democratic Front in the Women's Union secretariat, said Arafat even rejected internal substitutions sent by her faction. She herself had not wanted to go, preferring to focus on her party work in the Jordanian People's Party, which is the Democratic Front's official party there.

The 20th session was held at the Palace of Conferences where the National Council had previously met. The palace stood in safety in the secluded Snobar (pine) area, among green hills several miles away from the bustle of Algiers. Delegates, official observers, and journalists were transported from hotels in the area and from the city and did not return until late evening. In the Mediterranean waters below stood an Algerian navy ship at guard, its radar antennas in view.

The PLO leadership, including Fateh's Yasser Arafat, Popular Front's George Habash, and Nayef Hawatmeh and Yasser Abed Rabbo, heads of the two wings of the recently splintered Democratic Front, stayed in well-guarded nearby villas. The split in the Democratic Front reflected disagreement over Arafat's peace initiative, with Abed Rabbo aligned with Arafat, and the faction's general secretary Hawatmeh maintained the party's traditional position of not negotiating with Israel until it accepted the idea of a Palestinian state with its capital in East Jerusalem.

Anecdotal accounts of the meeting indicated that routine business of the council's ten standing committees was kept to a minimum. Um Jihad noticed that the attendance at the one she chaired, the Social and Health Affairs Committee, was less than usual and that business went quickly.

Abu Ali sat in the audience of the Judicial Committee, which discussed the proposal for a Palestinian Justice Department. (The decision for new PLO departments was made at the 19th session in 1988 and was meant to prepare for statehood.) Abu Ali asked the Judicial Committee to create an office of family relations in the proposed department and was assured that "of course, it would be included."

Abu Ali, who had been in Fateh's women's leadership since the beginning of the national movement, was not so convinced. In 1975, Abu Ali wrote the first book about the participation of women in the Palestinian movement, in which she observed that little progress was being made. When asked why she did not write another account, she responded that she would "when I feel there is something new." Abu Ali, however, hoped that maybe the Intifada was changing some of the attitudes toward women.

In other business, the National Council voted to add three additional seats to the Executive Committee, bringing the total to eighteen. This was to accommodate the split in the Democratic Front between the faction led by Hawatmeh and the one led by Abed Rabbo, and to introduce more independents and technocrats. However, none of the newcomers was a woman.

The undeniable candidate was Um Jihad, who sat in Fateh's Central Committee and was head of the Families of the Martyrs foundation. However, the problem has always been that Fateh's share of the seats was already filled by Abu Mazen, Abu Lutuf, and Arafat. The recent expansion, however, gave Um Jihad hope that a seat for women could be added. This was a clear departure from her thinking in the 1960s, when she was against having a separate women's cadre organization in Fateh or a designated women's representative in the PLO leadership.

Um Jihad had informally tested the ground and found no resistance from the women of the Popular and Democratic fronts. But she had not tried to solicit the official support of the Women's Union. In any case, the timing for advancing her to the Executive Committee was inopportune. Arafat would most certainly have vetoed the idea because it would have upset the precious factional balance he carefully guarded. As it was, the topic of the hour was the upcoming Middle East Peace Conference, which occupied everyone's attention.

As in almost all previous sessions, the National Council had the urgent task of putting a seal of legitimacy on Arafat's new course for the PLO. Arafat had asked the Council to agree to a joint Palestinian-Jordanian delegation to go to the Middle East Peace Conference without preconditions or guarantees—and without direct participation by the PLO. Furthermore, the Palestinian representatives to the conference were to be selected from inside the territories. It was a difficult pill for the National Council to swallow but, Arafat argued, it was necessary to bring Israel and the United States to the negotiating table with the PLO. It was a crucial vote for Arafat, one that would send word to the world and, more importantly, to internal critics that the Palestinians were behind him.

The political situation was especially ripe for Arafat's daring move. The Intifada, which had entered its fourth year, created much-needed leverage with Israel, and PLO resources were extremely strained with the loss of Gulf Arab funding in penalty for the PLO's opposition to the war on Iraq. There was also the Islamist double sword of Hamas (Arabic, acronym for Islamic Resistance Movement, literally means zeal) and Islamic Jihad out of Gaza, threatening both the secular, pluralistic PLO and Israel. Hamas and Islamic Jihad are the two organizations leading the Islamic resurgence in the Occupied Territories. The Islamist movement began in the late 1970s, first in the Gaza Strip and later spreading throughout the territories as Hamas, in particular, took a leading role in the Intifada. Arafat was in the process of pulling off one more coup in his pursuit of a political solution, the route he studiously followed since the promulgation of the Provisional Solution at the 12th National Council in 1974.

Arafat's proposal was considered by the Political Committee, chaired by one of its staunch proponents, Fateh's Nabil Sha'ath. The opposition was centered in the Popular Front and the Democratic Front's faction led by Hawatmeh—but there was opposition from many sides. The opposition stood for Israeli guarantees of full withdrawal from the 1967 Occupied Territories, including East Jerusalem, as a precondition for peace negotiations. The debate was heated in committee as it was later on the floor.

The delegates from the women's leadership concurred that open debate was part of the culture of the National Council. Some noticed it was especially so in the 19th and 20th sessions. But several were also critical, referring to "rigid partisanship," "Arab countries interference," and "members who just want to hear themselves speak." A Popular Front delegate said, "Yes, everyone speaks their mind but then Arafat makes the decision."

In the end, resolutions of the National Council were reached behind closed doors negotiated by the leaders of the factions that delivered the delegates in their respective teams. "Every faction member is bound by what the faction decides," said one from Fateh. "I mean, I can't go out and give an opinion that is in opposition to the Fateh faction because in the first degree we have a commitment to the faction."

The vote for the peace conference was 313 for and 18 against; it was unknown how many of the remaining delegates had abstained or were absent.[9] The women from the factions all voted with their groups; Women's Union president Abdel Hadi—who was an independent—was among those who voted against. (Abdel Hadi was among twenty-six members of the 106-member Central Council that, in 1993, sent a letter to Arafat voting against the Declaration of Principles; the final vote was 63 for, 8 abstaining, and a total of 35 against.)

The 20th session of the National Council was the last to be held in the diaspora (at the time of this writing, preparations have begun for holding the 21st session in Gaza). The National Council had maintained the facade of a mobilized Palestinian nation to the outside world but, in reality, since the late '70s the mobilizational work of the PLO in the diaspora was in steady and rapid retreat. And yet it was during the mobilizational stages in Jordan and Lebanon that women were able to develop and strengthen factional women's organizations, more active women's charitable societies, and the umbrella Women's Union. Women, however, never became a critical mass in the leadership ranks of the PLO. A few in the women's leadership were openly concerned about that, but understood that to fight for pay-offs for women's years of contributing to the movement would have meant serious and prolonged confrontations within their respective factions. The crisis-ridden political environment of the liberation struggle necessitated party loyalty and discipline and did not permit such maverick behavior on the part of the women. Generally, however, the women's leadership was restrained by the sobering realization that sexist social attitudes that allocated politics to men were as deeply entrenched in the thinking of the factions as in the general Palestinian population.

The final decision that paved the way for the Palestinians to attend the Madrid conference was made in mid-October 1991, when both the Executive Committee and the Central Council authorized the joint Jordanian-Palestinian representation. The Palestinian delegation from the Occupied Territories was on its way to Madrid for the peace conference that began on October 30, 1991.

The peace negotiations that subsequently were held in Washington D.C. brought Hanan Ashrawi into the limelight as spokeswoman for the Palestinian delegation. Ashrawi, who was a dean at Birzeit University in the West bank, first came into prominence a few months after the Intifada erupted, when she participated in a three-hour groundbreaking Israeli-Palestinian debate, televised by the American Broadcasting Corporation program "Nightline" in April 1988. She had mostly worked as an academic and had little previous history in PLO politics.

VII.

Ashrawi, PLO Ambassador Shahid, and others are a new breed of leaders who rose to high-ranking posts in the PLO in the late 1980s. They are a segment of the third generation of leading women who live mainly in the diaspora and are employed by the PLO's political departments: the Political Department (foreign affairs), the National Relations Department, and the Office of the General Commander (Arafat's office). The other segment in the third generation leads in women's organizations mainly inside the Occupied Territories.

Ashrawi and her colleagues had some mobilizational experience earlier on but came into prominence as part of the Western-oriented thrust of the PLO and the peace process. Their strength might be summed up as the ability to communicate with both Western and Israeli audiences. These women are highly educated (almost all have graduate degrees) and started as young activists in the 1970s in the socially-tolerant Paris and Beirut—where Ashrawi, who is from the West Bank, had also gone to attend the American University. Their political careers were shaped outside the Women's Union framework in the PLO's political departments and offices, sometimes called the "men's tract" for political advancement. Almost all the women in this group started their political involvement at university through the Union of Palestine Students. (In fact, a preponderant number of PLO diplomats date their entry into the national movement through university activism.) After graduation, the women worked mainly in Palestinian research and public information institutions such as the Institute of Palestine Studies in Paris—the political training ground of Ambassador Shahid. They are the part of the PLO's ranks that is as comfortable in Paris, Washington D.C., and London as they are in Jerusalem, Tunis, and Cairo.

They work directly under the PLO's top leadership, which makes them an important part of the PLO's decision-making apparatus. In the words of Salwa Mustafa, who lives in Tunis and works for the Department of National Relations:

It is a general principle, I mean, I have this opinion that the most important position is the one who gives the decision maker the capability to make the decision. It is the position situated around the center of the decision itself. It is the one who prepares the dossiers, collects the information and prepares the file for the leader. It is not necessary that one be a member of the Executive Committee as long as one participates in the work of making the decisions.

Mustafa is a Tunisian married to a Palestinian, Hisham Mustafa, who is an aid to Abu Mazen, head of the Department of National Relations and a Fateh member of the PLO Executive Committee. The Mustafas had met in France, where they were students organizing Palestine solidarity committees among the large Algerian labor force there.

However, in contrast to staying in the women's sphere, working in the male-dominated offices meant additional pressures, as oftentimes the women had to contend with sexual innuendo. Living away from Palestinian concentrations in Tunis or Europe produced a certain degree of liberalization in gender relationships, but some men interpreted liberalization as permission to trespass into inappropriate sexual behavior. That is why women generally had to rely on the "protection" of a father, a husband, or a brother. Attaching oneself to an unrelated man as a patron also worked, but sometimes backfired because people were apt to suspect a romantic involvement.

The sexual reputation issue was especially sensitive when one worked late hours, risking flaunting Arab norms against women staying out late at night. Sulafa Hijawi had to face this issue when she began to work with Arafat, who is known for his night-long schedule. Hijawi is actually an old hand in the Palestinian movement, as founder of both the Palestinian Women's Union and the Writers' and Journalists' Union branches in Iraq, where she had taught political science for many years at Baghdad University. In Tunis, she worked in Arafat's General Commander office as an advisor with unspecified assignments. She said the problem was not Arafat, with whom she felt very comfortable, but with the free-floating gossip that could have damaged her reputation as a woman. It was this sort of concern with one's sexual reputation that discouraged many women from working in mixed-gender settings in PLO offices. Karma Nabulsi, who worked for a time as second in command of the PLO office in London, pointed out that women tended to stay with the Women's Union "because it is safe."

Hijawi, Mustafa and the others in this elite group of women work in small teams, or individually, mainly behind the scenes. They have an entrepreneurial style of operating, typical of Fateh (though not all are from that faction). For example, Mustafa is part of a husband-wife team inside a four-person Israeli Affairs office in the Department of National Relations. This team works directly with Abu Mazen who, in September 1993, in Washington, D.C., signed the Declaration of Principles on behalf of the PLO. Abu Mazen, Abu Ala', and Nabil Sha'ath are men on the Palestinian side who greatly helped to bring about the agreement with Israel. In 1990, the Israeli Affairs office was already engaged in informal communications with American Jews and private Israelis in order to solicit support for peace based on the two-state solution, launched at the National Council's 19th session in 1988. One of the first such meetings was with a private American Jewish delegation in Stockholm in 1988, attended by Hisham Mustafa, husband of Salwa Mustafa.[10] Meetings with Israelis were also initiated, said Salwa Mustafa, who simply remarked, "We needed to listen to them."

Since the late 1980s, all the women in the PLO's political departments were engaged in varying degrees in the strategy to redefine the Palestinian movement to the Western and Israeli mainstream publics. The challenge was to alter the PLO's image from that of a radical, anti-Western organization to one that focused on peace and human rights. It was a goal made possible by the new political realities created by the resilience of the 1987 Intifada in the Occupied Territories and the increasing number of Israelis who wanted a peaceful resolution to the conflict with the Palestinians.

VIII.

In May 1989, Ashrawi, Hijawi, Shahid, and Naufal participated in the Brussels conference. This was an all-women meeting of fifty Palestinians and Israelis from the mainstream of both communities. The Palestinians included political independents, members of Fateh, the Democratic Front, and the Palestine Communist Party; the Popular Front, which did not want to participate in the peace process, was not represented. The Israelis consisted of women's rights' and peace activists, including some from the Labor Party. The setting was safe and comfortable at David and Simone Sisskind's Jewish Secular Cultural Community Center. The meetings continued for a week and into all hours of the night.

The Brussels meeting was groundbreaking in two ways. It was the first-ever open meeting between members of the Israeli establishment and representatives of the PLO in the diaspora. Prior to that time, some of the women from the Occupied Territories and from the Israeli peace camp had engaged in meetings, but these were mostly informal. Brussels also brought together women from the women's and men's tracts on each side of the conflict. The names of some of the participants, in addition to those from Tunis, are indicative of what was accomplished.

Among the Israeli participants were MK (member of Knesset) Shulamit Aloni, leader of the Citizen's Rights' Movement; MK Nava Arad from the Labor party; Yael Dayan, who is a writer, activist, and daughter of Israeli war hero Moshe Dayan, also from Labor; Maryam Mar'i, who is a well-known Arab-Israeli community leader and founder and director of the Early Childhood Education Center for the Arab Child in Acre; Alice Shalvi, who is head of the Israeli Women's Network, which tried to pool both leftist and mainstream women to work on women's issues; and Hebrew University political scientist Naomi Chazan.

The Occupied Territories' team included a Democratic Front leader, Zahira Kamal, who is also a founder of the Women's Committees' Movement and president of the Women's Action Committees; Rana Nashashibi, one of the leaders of communist Working Women's Committees; Salwa Hdeib from Fateh's Social Work Committees; and Mary Khass, who headed UNRWA's Childhood Development Center in Gaza. Also attending were three Palestinian academics from Birzeit University: Hanan Ashrawi, who taught English literature, Su'ad Amri who taught architecture, and community health professor and leading activist Rita Giacaman.

Before the women went home, they issued a seven-point declaration. They agreed that both Israelis and Palestinians should share the land "based on the principle of territorial separation" (point one); that "all peoples in the region have the right to live in freedom, dignity, and security (point four); that "each party in the conflict has the legitimate right to determine its own representatives" (point five); and that negotiations should be held under international auspices (point six). The Palestinians had wanted to use the phrase "peace process" but settled for "negotiations" to appease MK Arad, who insisted on using the one used by her party in its platform for the 12th Knesset. The astonishing thing was that the 1989 meeting revealed agreement on some of the most important items of contention between the PLO and Israel.[11]

Brussels also registered the fact that the Intifada had propelled women toward more visible public roles as speakers and negotiators. Participant Mar'i noted later that the conference had the effect of boosting women from the community service sphere into "official politics." This was dramatically apparent in the new posts some of these women acquired.

On the Israeli side, Aloni came on board Prime Minister Yitzhak Rabin's cabinet—the reward for her party's success in the 1992 Israeli elections and its coalition with Labor; Chazan and Dayan also won seats to the

Knesset. On the Palestinian side, three of the participants at Brussels became part of the Palestinian contingent to the Middle East Peace Conference; Ashrawi, as behind the scenes negotiator and official spokeswoman, Amri as negotiator, and Kamal as official advisor. In 1994, Kamal was given by Arafat the women's portfolio in the Palestinian National Authority.

Chairman Arafat also revealed in his speech at the National Press Club in Washington, D.C. (September 14, 1993) that two of the women from the Brussels group, Aloni and Ashrawi (along with Palestinian poet Mahmoud Darwish), participated in back-channel meetings but that they did not pan out because of media leaks.

The full story of women's involvement in the Palestinian-Israeli peace negotiations will undoubtedly continue to be revealed in interesting bits of information. The Brussels meeting, however, gave a clear signal that leadership among the Palestinian women evolved from several roles and settings that extended not only from Tunis and other Arab capitals but also from East Jerusalem.

Chapter 5

JERUSALEM
Women's Committees in the Occupied Territories

I.

On March 8, 1984, Israeli soldiers set up a roadblock at the Ram intersection on the Jerusalem-Ramallah Road in the West Bank. Ram is one of the Palestinian towns and villages that extend from the suburbs of Jerusalem in a residential chain north to al-Bireh and Ramallah. The intersection at the entrance to the town is a familiar checkpoint, used by the Israeli Defense Forces to close off Jerusalem to the rest of the Palestinians living in the West Bank.

The task for the soldiers was extraordinary that day, for it said to order back Palestinian women and children. The Palestinians were on their way to attend festivities held in and around Jerusalem to honor International Women's Day. The Israeli military authorities, holding the West Bank and Gaza Strip since 1967, knew that International Women's Day had become a yearly occasion where the PLO recognized Palestinian women. The soldiers, however, were not completely successful for on that day and the next, hundreds of Palestinian women and children circumvented the roadblock by using out-of-the-way roads to get to Jerusalem, and celebrations were held all over the West Bank. Jerusalem's Palestinian newspaper *al-Fajr*, noting the barring of the women, then proceeded to report on the festivities in Jerusalem, Ramallah and al-Bireh cities and in the Dheisheh refugee camp in Bethlehem.[1]

The celebrations included the familiar spectrum of Palestinian political festivals, but it was also apparent that a great deal of preparation had gone into the programs. The newspaper said the audiences heard speeches about the current political situation and about the changing roles of women. Participants listened to commemorations of local martyrs and messages sent by political prisoners. The entertainment included folk dancing, poetry, songs, and skits. Bazaars set up for the occasion sold traditional Palestinian embroidery. What the soldiers at the Ram intersection might not have realized was that International Women's Day also marked the birth of an unfolding Women's Committees' Movement that had begun six years earlier. It is not often that the birth of a social movement can be narrowed to a day and place.

The Women's Committees' Movement began at an afternoon meeting on March 8, 1978, in the old library in Ramallah in the West Bank. Some thirty women, all from the urban middle class in the Jerusalem and Ramallah areas, came to discuss how women could be organized to support the steadfastness effort. Steadfastness was the Palestinian buzzword for peaceful resistance against the Israeli occupation, and by the early '70s it had replaced the collapsed armed struggle movement in the West Bank and Gaza Strip. The women at the Ramallah library meeting were familiar faces to one another, as they worked together in the community volunteers' movement that was taking shape in the mid-1970s. To an outsider, the library meeting would have been innocuous; the idea of women doing volunteer work was as old as their great grandmothers who had started charitable societies as early as 1902 in Acre on the Mediterranean coast. A closer look would have revealed the nucleus of the Occupied Territories' incoming second and third generations of women's leadership. These were enthusiastic young cadres who were in their 20s and early 30s and ready to make their mark for the Palestinian cause.

At the center was second-generation Democratic Front's Zahira Kamal who, with fellow partisan Siham Barghouti, issued the invitation for the meeting and would soon form the Women's Action Committees. Also greatly interested was young Maha Nassar, a leading student cadre for the Popular Front at nearby Birzeit University who later headed the Palestinian Women's Committees. The other two leaders of unions of women's committees were not at the meeting—Fateh's Rabiha Diab was in prison, and communist Amal Khriesheh was in Amman studying psychology at the Jordanian University. However, at the meeting were women from all the major PLO factions and several independents. The Ramallah library meeting concluded by setting up the first Women's Volunteer Work Committee. It was a modest step that no one at the time could have predicted would lead to a women's political movement.

The turning point in Palestinian resistance to the Israeli occupation was the 1976 municipal elections that were held throughout the Occupied Territories. This was the second time such elections had been held since the 1967 occupation and the first time the nationalist forces decided to participate. Until the 1993 Israeli-PLO accord came into effect, the enfranchisement of Palestinians of the Occupied Territories was a rare occasion indeed. The Arabs of East Jerusalem were the exception because East Jerusalem was annexed by Israel and its residents could vote in the unified Jerusalem's municipal elections, but they tended to boycott elections in protest of the occupation. The 1976 West Bank municipal elections provided a great opportunity for the PLO to show its support among the people, and its candidates, who ran as the unified nationalist slate, were victorious, toppling the traditional political leadership of Jordanian-supported mayors and village chiefs.[2]

At the time of the 1976 elections, however, there were no mass organizations to channel the political energies of activist women. Female university students were active in organizing and leading student unions, especially at Birzeit University, the well-known nationalist school located just north of Ramallah. The PLO Women's Union was illegal and inactive but clandestinely headed by Samiha Khalil, who was also president of In'ash al-Usra, the charitable society she had formed in 1965.

Khalil rose to national stature during the period 1978–1982 as a member of the short-lived National Guidance Committee, which consisted of mayors, representatives of mass organizations, and charitable societies in the West Bank and Gaza Strip. The committee was organized to mount a protest against the 1979 Israeli-Egyptian Peace Treaty, which was seen as fundamentally flawed. The treaty, which primarily dealt with returning Sinai (occupied in 1967) to Egypt and an Egyptian-Israeli peace, incurred the anger of the Palestinians for two main reasons. One, it neutralized Egypt, which had been one of their staunchest allies and, two, it glossed over the issue of returning the Occupied Territories, with a vague promise of autonomy to the residents; in all it was a slap to the Palestinian dream of self-determination and statehood.[3]

Khalil's power base was the proliferating charitable societies' movement, which carried most of the weight of caring for the poor under the occupation. The charitable field was the political arena of first-generation women, which was how, many years later, they contributed to the steadfastness movement.[4] Steadfastness meant bolstering Palestinian institutions such as universities and research centers, community health clinics, and labor and professional unions.

Palestinian women voted in the 1976 municipal elections but were not placed on the PLO's ticket. According to Rima Nasser Tarazi of the In'ash al-Usra Society, the national forces did not want to give Israel a propaganda point to say it helped liberate Palestinian women. But the 1976 elections signalled the ascendence of second- and third-generation PLO men and women from labor and professional unions, and the universities.[5] And, by the early '80s, four faction-sponsored women's unions came unto the scene, which organized the International Women's Day celebrations in 1984.

The first three groups represent the leftist current in the Palestinian liberation movement and, in contrast with the mobilization in the diaspora of the 1970s when Fateh dominated, the leftists led in organizing women in the West Bank and Gaza Strip.

The oldest group is the Union of Women's Action Committees, established in 1978. Its founder and president is Zahira Kamal, who was the leading figure in the Democratic Front in the Occupied Territories until it split into two; she is now a leader of the Palestinian Democratic Union Party (Fida), Yasser Abed Rabbo's group. For most of its history, the Women's Action focused its recruitment on housewives, who constituted 75 percent of the membership. In 1992, however, the leadership decided to expand its appeal to include employed women. The union's membership reached a height of 10,000 in 1990, before splitting in half in 1991 because of the schism inside its sponsoring faction, the Democratic Front, over the peace process.

The Union of Palestinian Women's Committees, affiliated with the Popular Front, was established in 1981; its leader is Maha Nassar. The size of the union's membership is kept secret, but it is estimated to have 5,000 to 6,000 members, with a high proportion of students.

The Union of Working Women's Committees was also established in 1981 and is led by Amal Khriesheh. The union, which is sponsored by the Palestine Communist Party (now the Palestine People's Party), initially focused on working women and students; its membership reached a height of 5,000. After 1990, however, the union's grassroots organizing faltered because of lack of funds and the collapse of the Soviet block. Consequently, the Union's leading women became more independent from the Communist Party and are interested in a variety of women's rights' issues.

The last group to form was the Union of Social Work Committees, which was established in 1982 and is led by Rabiha Diab. The union is affiliated with Fateh and its membership is diverse and growing, having reached 8,000 women in 1990.

These four unions represent the tour de force of the second and third generations of leaders.[6] These data, from 1990, symbolize the ability of women from the main PLO factions to navigate past Israeli suppression of political activity in the Occupied Territories. Also, in creating their own organizations, these cadres had made a declaration of independence from the charitable work of their mothers' generation.

II.

The second- and third-generation women's leadership in the Occupied Territories, as their comrades in the diaspora, were never satisfied with charitable work and most, especially those in the third generation, did not partake in it. They were children of the '60s and '70s who believed in social change and thought charitable work elitist, holding little promise of changing the oppressive situation of Arab women. They were daughters of Nasser's Arab nationalism and the Palestinian National Movement, and at university were rapidly drawn to student activism organized by the Popular and Democratic fronts, the Palestine Communist Party, and Fateh.[7]

The women were respectful of their mothers' generation. "This is something one cannot ignore," said third-generation Nassar, head of the Palestinian Women's Committees. "They gave and sacrificed and still do; they are part of the women's movement." Second-generation Kamal of the Women's Action Committees and first-generation societies leader Khalil were also reportedly good friends, which might have been due to the fact that Kamal and at least one of Khalil's sons were leaders in the Democratic Front.

To Khalil's generation, the women from the factions were the "young ones" who were less cautious and who could, at times, be a little dangerous. For a long time, the women's sphere in the nationalist movement was able to escape the heavy-handed Israeli military administration because their work was perceived to be social not political. However, some in the societies feared that the political organizations set up by the younger generations brought unwanted attention that could disrupt the lifelong work of the charitable societies.

And they had cause to worry, for the young leaders of the Women's Committees' Movement were veterans of Israeli political imprisonment. Branded by Israel as "members of an enemy organization," they were frequent guests at Jerusalem's Russian Interrogation Compound, Nablus's Central Prison, and the women's prison, Neve Tirze. Head of the Social Work Committees, Diab, spent several years in prison, and Kamal of the Women's Action Committees was briefly jailed and under sun-up to sundown house arrest for seven years (until 1987). Nassar of the Palestinian Women's Committees was only nineteen when she was first taken away for interrogation, and on the second arrest, she recalled, her mother was less fearful: "Prison is for men," she said—meaning for the brave.

The women's leadership in the Occupied Territories was first and foremost nationalist and it saw equality between men and women possible only after statehood. For the centrists of the women's societies and Fateh, the social agenda had to wait. Societies' leader Khalil of In'ash al-

Usra said, "Now if we want to get our political rights we need to have elections. If we want to change the law for women's rights, who do we address?" Fateh's Diab of the Social Work Committees concurred, saying: "Of course, the woman should have the same personal freedom as the man. The current state of the struggle does not permit me to give first attention or full attention to this matter."

Leaders of the three leftist unions of women's committees believed that social change for women must be part of the nationalist agenda. Khriesheh of the Working Women's Committees and Kamal of the Women's Action Committees affiliated with historically Marxist-Leninist groups (the Palestine Communist Party and the Democratic Front), but in their own views they had long departed from strict class analysis and were self-defined feminists. In the words of Khriesheh:

> We not only want simply political rights but also to use political rights to get our social rights. She (the woman) should have the right to choose who she marries and divorces, whether to finish her education. She should have the right—let me call it—to practice her humanity.

Legal equality was paramount in their thinking, but they understood that it could only be truly achieved when a consensus for social change developed in the culture. This was also the view of Marxist-Leninist Nassar of the Palestinian Women's Committees (of the Popular Front.) She was especially vehement in saying that the battle for rights must not be defined as anti-male. She said:

> I don't see the Palestinian women's movement in conflict with the Palestinian man in any of the issues. If we discuss the male we need to discuss him as part of the oppressive backward society, the whole society. The Palestinian man in general is not the enemy. We hear about extremists to the degree that they describe their program as anti-men and they have clubs and signs that say "no men allowed." I saw that in Europe. We Palestinians, we will never have clubs special for women and celebrations for women only or deviant relations between women and things like that. These demands fundamentally do not suit our society and we will not permit them ever.

Kamal agreed, saying: "The question sometimes is not a question of the woman and the man. The woman can be more oppressive than the man—I mean of the woman. What is important is the ideas that the woman has." The three leftist groups were especially keen on making changes in how women thought of themselves in relation to the Palestinian movement and their own status in the society.

It was all reminiscent of the leftists in the diasporan women's leadership in Lebanon, but the political environment had changed. In place of the whirlwind of the Lebanese civil war, there was a new political order that unfolded in the 1987 uprising, the rise of Hamas, and the PLO's diplomatic maneuvers, culminating in the PLO-Israeli accord of September 1993, the Declaration of Principles.

III.

The hubs of Palestinian politics in the Occupied Territories are located along the Jerusalem-Ramallah-Nablus urban nexus of the West Bank, and Gaza city in the Strip. The two centers are separated by a single 100 km two-lane highway through Israel. The women's leadership lived in and around Jerusalem, and that is where it started to organize.

About one-third of all Palestinians live in the West Bank and Gaza Strip and, of those, two-fifths are refugees.[8] The Bank is home to two-thirds of the Palestinians living in the Occupied Territories and it is also larger and more spread out than the Strip. The West Bank is 130 km north to south and 30–40 km east to west, while the Gaza Strip is only 44 km in length and 4–12 km in width. The vast majority of the 495 Palestinian villages in the Occupied Territories are located in the Bank, which also has twenty refugee camps. The camps can be found throughout, but about half of the people in them live in the Nablus area, which is 65 km north of Jerusalem. The city also hosted the largest and most politically volatile camp, Balata. Altogether, about one-fourth of West Bankers are refugees. The many villages and camps in the Bank reminds one of the reality that the Occupied Territories are at once home to those with ancestral roots in the area and are a place of exile for the refugees.

The Gaza Strip is logistically less accessible to the women's leadership in the West Bank. As the southern tip of Palestine, it is closer to Egypt, which administered it in the 1948–1967 period. The population of the Strip is concentrated in three cities—Gaza, Khan Unis and Rafah—and in eight refugee camps and a few villages. Both the Bank and the Strip have suffered from frequent curfews and telephone cut-offs, disrupting communications between the two regions. The Strip, however, could also be easily cordoned off by a single roadblock at the Eretz checkpoint at the entrance to Gaza.

The Gaza Strip is also a greatly distressed community. It is distinguished by having one of the highest population densities in the world (an average of 1,800/sq. km. and as high as 5,000/sq. km. around Gaza city).[9] In 1948 the Strip was already one of Palestine's poorest regions when it lost much of its agricultural land to Israel.[10] At the same time, it was inundated with refugees who now constitute two-thirds of its residents. The scarcity of resources and the political situation meant high unemployment, especially among the refugees, half of whom still live in the Strip's eight refugee camps. (It is in the largest of these camps, Jabalya, on the outskirts of Gaza that the Intifada began.) Underneath its often curfewed streets, Gaza conveyed an air of combustion ripe with nationalist and conservative sentiments. This was Fateh and Hamas country.[11] There is a degree of desperation and anger in Gaza, unlike any other place; it is the greatest reminder of the Palestinian tragedy. Consequently, Gazans have always been great trouble to the Israeli occupation administration, which is why Israel wanted to unload it fast onto the PLO's shoulders.

Gaza's social, economic, and political environment presented the women's leadership out of the West Bank with an ambiguous environment for women's mobilization. Gaza is a society that embraced its children who resisted the occupation, including the females among them. Local Democratic Front leader Ne'meh Helou (unrelated to Jihan and Shadia), who was sought by Israel for membership in the Unified Leadership of the Uprising (the secret leadership of the Intifada), was able to go into hiding for years. Helou was Kamal's counterpart in Gaza and a former commando who spent the '70s in prison, and upon release did mobilization work for her faction. (In 1990, shortly after I met her, she was arrested and remained in prison until she was released in 1993, following the Israeli-PLO accord.) Now she is the top woman in the Palestinian Democratic Union Party in the Gaza Strip and in her party's congress in 1995; she received the most votes for leadership among both female and male candidates. Gaza is also a conservative society—not very hospitable to attempts to liberalize women's roles and that attitude hindered the recruitment drive of the Women's Committees' Movement.

The Palestinian social landscape is generally conservative and economically distressed throughout the Territories, as it is in the refugee camps of the diaspora, so organizers had to address in Gaza and elsewhere the very same constraints on women's resources. Especially stark were women's low levels of education and economic dependency. For example, in 1987, the average housewife had less than nine years of school.[12] This was especially a problem in the villages, where advancing above the elementary level often meant commuting outside one's village or town, which produces fears for their girls' reputations. In the refugee camps, UNRWA has schools for both boys and girls and most of the camps are located near cities, making education more accessible. The refugees also placed a great value on education for both sexes, as the only way out of poverty.[13] Once out of school, however, the vast majority of women tended to marry and only a small minority engaged in employment.

As was the case in the diasporan organizing effort during the Jordanian and Lebanese periods, recruits were approached through the usual social rituals, and organizers found inroads by providing assistance and friendship. In the words of an organizer for the Social Work Committees in Gaza:

> We usually try to reach the woman in her home, right in her place. We do not burden her to have to come to us. For example, I have a neighbor whose son was arrested, I then go to her at the house and tell her to give me his name and the number of his identity card and I go inform the Cross (International Red Cross). I do not wish to give her the burden of this work. No, on the contrary, I want to make her feel that her son is like my brother. For sure, most of the aware sisters work like this.

For the three leftist groups, success required turning away from the Marxist-Leninist secret cells to the more open structure of volunteer committees. Sometimes it was also necessary to secure the support of the male elders in some of the more tightly woven village communities. It was difficult at times to gain the trust of the people. An organizer for the Women's Action Committees in Nablus said:

> Sometimes the woman becomes afraid. She agrees to join the committees but she returns after two to three days or a week and says, "My husband wouldn't let me" or "I am afraid because you belong to a certain political current." We try to convince her that it is her right to join a political program, even if her political inclinations are somewhere else. [We say] "you can be an active member in this framework in a very ordinary way and it is not necessary that you become obligated."

A Gazan in charge of the Middle Camps for the Women's Action Committees, gave a step-by-step account of how a women's committee would be started.[14] She said:

> We go at first to the house to visit one who is receptive to be active in the committees. She gathers the women around her. She brings them one of us who has a good idea about the program. We present the program of the committees. We present what the role of women is, how we will develop ourselves and how we will take part in the national struggle, which cannot be separated from the social struggle to improve women's social and eco-

nomic conditions. . . . After that, through our discussion—there are many people who speak and ask for explanation—we sense who is enthusiastic of the twenty, thirty, or thirty-five who attended. [They ask] "How could one work?"

The organizer would then take this opportunity to suggest forming a local women's committee. She would say, "I am from outside the neighborhood and couldn't come to you. The one who should work with you should be one, two or a group of you. So why don't you choose one or two of you to represent you." Afterwards, other meetings are arranged and a local committee is born. In the words of the Gazan organizer:

After that we return and have another meeting, and another, and we explain to them the basic structures of the union. We choose from them five or seven, depending on the number present—the most enthusiastic group—and we delegate to them the basic responsibility for the activities, calling meetings and so on.

Organized day trips were occasions for interested women from different areas to meet and get away from their daily routines but, occasionally, participants had to deal with harassment from some of the men standing by in the streets. Kamal said these encounters proved to be good opportunities for leadership training, and gave the example of an excursion her group once organized for women from several West Bank villages. Kamal said some of the men in one village met the tour bus and said none of "our women" will go. Kamal answered them: "Okay, we shall drive around in town and we shall take those who join us." This they did and the outcome was a success; they had registered for one bus and ended filling up two. Kamal said:

We knew how to work with the local society, I mean, instead of leaving at seven we left at nine because it took us time to debate. But in the end, the women themselves stood firm because they wanted to go on the trips. . . . And now we have in those locations, where we faced great difficulties, the strongest of our sites. And they have great perseverance, they have high potential, very big, and they have abilities in persuasion.

Hanan Ashrawi, who lived in Ramallah, West Bank, was a longtime observer of the Women's Committees' Movement. In her opinion, the entry of the women's committees into the villages was a tremendous breakthrough in the nationalist effort to involve women:

I think they are more successful than we think they are because they have managed to reach women in remote areas, women

who were hitherto neglected, who were not part of the nationalist or feminist movements. And by creating work opportunities,
by getting them involved, by giving them the channels, the
avenues for self-expression and decision-making, they have
politicized women even beyond their wildest dreams—because
women were ready.

The three leftist groups, the Women's Action Committees, the
Palestinian Women's Committees, and the Working Women's Committees, led the way in recruitment, though they were mainly successful in
the West Bank. After the Intifada, however, the fortunes of the fourth
group, the Social Work Committees, began to improve when its sponsor
Fateh increased its funding, as evidenced by the many kindergartens it
opened during the period 1990–1991.

IV.

In the best tradition of Palestinian political factionalism, the four women's
unions competed along familiar lines. They organized adult literacy
classes for women (in a region where three-quarters of women forty-five
years and older had no formal schooling of any kind), and offered vocational workshops in sewing, weaving and such; but mostly, they competed with kindergartens. Each union had dozens of these one- to
three-room kindergartens that became the most visible measure of their
success.

The kindergartens did two things, said Abla Abu Elbi, a third-generation member of the Women's Union secretariat, who works out of the
office of the Jordanian People's Party in Amman. Abu Elbi was in close
contact with her group (the Democratic Front) across the border.
Kindergartens served women who were already active and needed child
care but they also provided an opportunity, she said, "To enter the location in which kindergartens are set up so as to enter a relationship with
the masses in those locations."

In the mid-1980s, two of the unions—the Palestinian Women's
Committees and the Women's Action Committees—experimented with
small-scale income-generating projects. Almost all involved food preservation, drawing on Arab women's traditional knowledge of homemade
preserves.

The Palestinian Women's Committees organized a few profit-sharing
cooperatives. Their two main projects were located in the villages of Sa'ir
(Hebron district) and Beitillo (Ramallah district). With about twenty-five
to thirty women each, they produced and marketed preserves, pickles,
jams, and fruit drinks. The Norwegian Save the Children Fund and the

Refugee Council provided the funds and Birzeit University provided the technical training.[15]

The central leadership of the Palestinian Women's Committees initiated the projects and arranged for technical assistance, then turned over business decisions regarding production, accounting, marketing, and distribution of profits to the participants. It was an interesting commentary on the times for the Marxist-Leninist-oriented leadership to opt for a semblance of capitalist thinking and recognize the profit motive. Theirs was a social democratic model, however. Eileen Kuttab was in charge of the development projects of the Palestinian Women's Committees. She said it was important to teach women that profits should be in part directed toward benefitting common interests—and gave the example of using a portion of the profit of the cooperative for a daycare center to serve the working mothers.

In contrast, the Women's Action Committees aimed at encouraging local initiative. Their two main village projects were the Abasan Biscuit and Milks center, located east of Khan Unis in the Gaza Strip, and the Essawiya Copper Works at the northeast end of Jerusalem. At Abasan, the local committee came up with the idea of making biscuits for commercial use and at first had to rely on a small conventional oven for the baking. The central office in Jerusalem was then asked for commercial equipment, which was eventually provided through funds from European development agencies.

The Essawiya Copper Works was a combined vocational training and income-generating project of the leadership of the Women's Action Committees. Started in early 1984, it was an experiment in nontraditional vocational education for young women, who were taught copper crafts. The idea was to teach them how to use hammers, wrenches, electric welders, and saws. "Men do these activities in our society," Kamal explained, "and now it is a new experience for women." Both unions saw their projects as catalysts of social change for the participating women. There was a consensus among the women's leadership in all the groups that making decisions at the workplace enhances a woman's self-confidence and is bound to affect her private life. It might mean, for example, simply being able to decide who she marries, rather than having to bend to her family's choice, as oftentimes happens in the more conservative families. The women's leadership, however, had no illusions that these isolated pilots would change social attitudes toward women's roles in the society. But they were small windows that the women in the villages could use to gain increased personal autonomy and self-initiative.

At the very beginning of the Palestinian National Movement, the hope of the leftists in the women's leadership was that women would become cadres in the factions and participate in the armed struggle. Now their goal was to provide models of how women could more widely be involved in Palestinian nation-building, however, they had to do so in ways that were unobtrusive to the prevailing social norms, for example, having more flexible work schedules and part-time work. (Interestingly, to be sensitive to the Muslim culture, the Women's Action Committees' magazine, *darb al-mar'a* (1991), contained a column by a Muslim scholar, who advised readers on women's rights in Islam.) "The work is enormous and requires great patience," Kamal said, and both the leadership of the Women's Action Committees and the Palestinian Women's Committees were in it for the long haul.

The Working Women's Committees' struggle was focused on women's labor rights—at best a frustrating enterprise. First, they could not, by law, unionize at sites across the Green Line (the 1948 border between Israel and the Occupied Territories). And it was there that thousands of female workers headed to fill low-paid agricultural and services jobs. Also, some of the women were difficult to reach because they were transported directly from their villages to Israel by special buses provided by the employers. Second, the Palestinian economy was greatly depressed because of Israeli policies against autonomous Palestinian development and because of high unemployment. Labor rights issues also took second seat to the national question, especially among the male-dominated labor unions that were often preoccupied with factional competitions.[16]

The Working Women's Committees led a couple of campaigns against Palestinian companies to win equal wages for women and to have International Women's Day be considered a paid holiday. Ashrawi was in the delegation that paid a visit to one of these factory owners:

> We formed a delegation of women across the board to go and defend women's rights and to demand equal wages and so we sent him word that we were coming. And when he found out that we were making an issue of it, immediately he said he changed. He gave in to the women.

She added, "We waged this as a feminist struggle rather than as a political group struggle." In the end, these successes were all symbolic without the mandate of law, but they were occasions—admittedly on a small scale— for the women's leadership to present a unified front on behalf of women's interests.

The Social Work Committees did not have a social-change agenda, which is consistent with its sponsor Fateh's purely national liberation purpose. The group had a few seasonal pickling projects such as one in the village of Kufr Malik (Ramallah district), but these were propelled by the

Intifada and were meant to symbolize one of its long-term goals for the Palestinians to disengage from the Israeli economy.[17]

V.

In the 1987 Intifada, known as "the uprising of the stones," Palestinian women were shown to Western audiences through television cameras. The images were of traditionally clad women breaking up boulders into smaller pieces thrown by the children, or shielding the children from Israeli soldiers. The women stood in the streets alongside boys (and sometimes girls), all challenging occupation soldiers with stones.

The Intifada lasted several years and was sustained by a wide infrastructure of organizations. Prior to 1987, it was common to have demonstrations and confrontations with the occupation forces against arrests, deportations, and other reminders of the occupation. The Intifada was different because of the prior development of women's, labor, and student unions, health clinics, and new universities, which sprung up in the late 1970s. The momentum of the Intifada meant the PLO's nation-building effort in the Occupied Territories had succeeded. But the Intifada was as much a statement of defiance and regained dignity as it was a message of acceptance that the home of the Palestinian state was to be limited to the West Bank and Gaza Strip. The Intifada also brought a greater visibility to the women's committees.

The Intifada gave the third generation their first taste of public exposure; other than Kamal, heads of women's committees were all from that generation. Women leaders were in demand as speakers at press conferences and at universities and other assemblies. The actual day-to-day leadership of the uprising, however, was in the hands of the secret Unified National Leadership of the Uprising, and it is not known if any women actually served in that body.

Women participated in the Intifada's Popular Committees that flourished at the outset, until they were banned in 1988 by the Israeli military administration. There were home teaching committees to substitute for the ordered-closed schools, emergency and health committees to help the wounded, and agricultural committees that experimented with growing food in neighborhood plots. However, women were visibly absent from guard duty committees, replacing local police who had resigned in support of the Intifada.[18]

Enthusiastic support for the uprising came from organized and unorganized women alike, but was ultimately sustained by widespread networks of Palestinian institutions—including women's committees and charitable societies. Women's organizations worked alongside worker and professional syndicates, student unions, merchants, and health service societies. They participated in distributing the secret communiques of the Unified Leadership, delivered PLO funds for social relief, visited prisoners and their families, and performed other activities that paralleled their sisters' work during the war in Lebanon.

Kamal felt extremely rewarded when she discovered that the women's committees in some of the remote villages remained viable during the weeks of curfews imposed by the military. She said:

> It showed that, indeed, our members were not waiting for the decision of the executive office. They were capable of taking decisions by themselves and of participating in the work according to the basic vision of the program and their understanding of it. Therefore, when we were able to return to see each other it was as if no interruption happened. I mean, all the work was according to the basic rules and this is something we are proud of, that we were able to realize it in spite of their difficult circumstances.

Generally, the different unions contributed separately except when coordinating the distribution of PLO funds given to families of prisoners and martyrs. These funds were channeled through the Higher Women's Council, the top leadership body that the women's committees' leadership founded in 1988 to provide just such coordination (actually, they had been meeting informally for much longer). In the language of Palestinian nationalism, the women's organizations "proved themselves" in the Intifada.

The PLO praised the women's organizations at the 19th National Council session in 1988. Muhammad Melhem, head of the PLO Department of the Affairs of the Occupied Homeland, said in his report to the Council:

> The events of the Intifada confirmed the central role of the popular frameworks: popular committees, women's and student's, professional and workers' unions, merchants' committees, societies and clubs, health committees and agricultural and others in the net of national institutions and popular frameworks that formed the arms of the national movement, its podiums and channels.

But the cost of women's higher visibility was high, as the detention and interrogation of activists intensified and some of their projects were attacked and their programs disrupted or destroyed.

During the Intifada, the income-generating projects went into crisis, burdened by a mix of political and economic impediments. As of 1993, the Beitillo cooperative was still unable to receive Israeli permission to build a larger facility, which the project needed if it was to become economically viable. The projects badly needed business expertise, especially in the area of modern marketing techniques, which apparently was the reason Abasan Biscuit had folded. It was also difficult to sustain the work and perform long-range planning with seasonal produce.

The effects of the Intifada on the Women's Committees' Movement were paradoxical. Women were politically visible in clashes with Israeli soldiers and in leadership podiums. The Intifada sparked enthusiasm that brought thousands to the women's committees, reaching an estimated height of 3 percent (28,000–29,000) of the Palestinian women in the Occupied Territories. The Palestinian women were engaged in politics as never before, and there was a feeling that they just might escape the specter of the Algerian women's experience. At the same time, the Intifada brought about a new political reality in the Occupied Territories that caused the Women's Committees' Movement to unravel.

VI.

The first signs of trouble appeared in Gaza in the summer of 1988. The city was experiencing the growth of Islamic fundamentalism, as embodied in the organizations of Hamas and Islamic Jihad. Gaza itself is not considered a sacred place in Islam, though it is special because it was home to Imam Shafi'i, the eighth-century founder of one of the four classical schools of Islamic jurisprudence, and not its strictest, in regards to family law and the treatment of women. Also, Prophet Muhammad's paternal great grandfather Hashim was buried in Gaza. But fundamentalism in Gaza had fed on the desperation of a people burdened by a great deal of unemployment and poverty, in an atmosphere of siege and nightly curfews (Jabalya and Shati refugee camps in particular had the disconcerting appearance of large concentration camps.)

Hamas and Islamic Jihad are offshoots of the Muslim Brotherhood, an Islamist organization founded in Egypt in 1928, with a broad agenda for return to Islamic principles by society and government. The Muslim Brothers came to Palestine in the late 1940s and fought as volunteers in support of the Palestinian cause in the 1948 War with the Jewish forces. During the period from the 1950s–1960s, the membership of the Muslim Brotherhood in the Arab world rose and fell, affected by the extent of support or suppression by Arab governments. In the West Bank and Gaza

Strip, however, the Palestinian branch of Muslim Brotherhood remained small, never reaching more than 2,000 in membership.[19]

In the 1970s, however, the Brotherhood and other Islamist revivalist groups benefitted by the rise of the Islamic fundamentalist movement that spread throughout the Arab and Islamic worlds. There is a general consensus that one of the most important causes that sparked Islamist activism was the 1967 Israeli victory over the Arabs, which was perceived as a humiliating defeat for Muslims. Another was the rise of the conservative Arab regimes of the Gulf area, especially Saudi Arabia, when their enormous wealth amassed from higher oil prices in the mid-to-late '70s, enabled them to exert influence throughout the Arab world. And, of course, there was the dramatic overthrow of the Shah of Iran by the Islamic forces in 1979.

The Islamist movement in the West Bank and Gaza Strip was visible in the dramatic growth of the number of mosques built since the 1970s and, also, in the proliferation of Islamic educational institutions, children's nurseries, youth clubs, health clinics, and vocational centers. This social service infrastructure, its heart the Muslim Brotherhood's Islamic Center in Gaza, took on a more overt political face only after the 1987 Intifada, and is mainly represented by Hamas. Islamic Jihad, founded in 1980, has had a fairly friendly relationship with the Fateh organization (though less so since the increase in Islamist violent attacks on Israeli targets during 1994 that challenged the PLO's dealings with Israel). In any case, Islamic Jihad is a rather small group. Hamas, on the other hand, represents the Palestinian resistance arm of the Muslim Brotherhood and was founded in 1987 as an active, militant alternative to the nationalist leadership. Hamas was poised to challenge the secular leadership of the PLO and especially Arafat's peace initiative and the two-state solution. To Hamas, Palestine is an Islamic *waqf* (trust), and no solution short of the full liberation of Palestine and a government of Islamic law, including a traditionalist social agenda, is acceptable.[20]

In the spring and summer of 1988, graffiti appeared everywhere in Gaza, calling for a return to modesty in dress and for women to wear the veil. Conservative attire, whether for religious reasons or just conforming to tradition, was already prevalent in Gaza, but now it would be mandated for political reasons. Hamas had decided women and adolescent girls must not appear in public without their heads and necks covered. This religious fundamentalist call was couched with nationalist rhetoric, telling women to veil and wear less colorful clothes to honor the martyrs of the Intifada.

Hamas's initiative found resonance in the mood of the city, where every neighborhood had seen death and injury. Social activities in Gaza had become more subdued as the human toll mounted; family outings by the sea disappeared, and marriage and birth celebrations were muted, as was the color of clothes.[21] How intently community supported Hamas is difficult to know. According to a public opinion poll in 1994, support for Hamas amounted to about 14 percent and, for Islamic Jihad, around 5 percent while the nationalist parties, especially Fateh, mustered a majority of the support.[22] In any case, the veil was enforced without regard to religious affiliation (in Gaza, Christians are a very small minority). There were reports of boys and young men verbally and physically harassing any defiant young women, who were hit with tomatoes, eggs, and stones. In at least one case, an unveiled women's committees' activist was hit with liquid acid. Also, some women's projects were attacked and a fire— that did little damage—was started at Abasan Biscuit.

In their turn, the women's committees offered no organized protest, and what little individual resistance there was came mainly from a few in the Palestinian Women's Committees. The well-known activist Itimad Mohanna, for example, was steadfast in her opposition to the veil and was reported as saying, "I shall not wear it even if I become martyr of the veil." (I saw Mohanna in 1990 at her newly established women's research center—then located at Gaza's Y.M.C.A.—and she was still unveiled.)

The leadership of the Palestinian Women's Committees, however, was of two minds about how to respond to the fundamentalist threat. Head of the union, Nassar, was unenthusiastic about battling Hamas because it would derail energies from the primary question of the occupation. Kuttab, who supervised the group's development projects, felt strongly that forced veiling could be the beginning of forcing women out of the public sphere. The Charter of Hamas said as much, when it declared that the woman's most important role was that of "taking care of the home and raising children of ethical character and understanding that comes from Islam. . ."[23]

The idea that Hamas used the veil as a symbol of its power vis-a-vis the PLO escaped none in the women's leadership in the Occupied Territories. But they all knew that fighting Hamas was a sensitive national question because it might fracture further an already fragile Palestinian consensus. Hamas's demand for the veil happened during the months surrounding the 19th National Council meeting in 1988. This was the session in which the PLO went on record in support of a Palestinian state in the Occupied Territories—in effect, giving up the liberation of all of Palestine. None of the PLO factions wanted a fight with Hamas now that the Palestinian National Movement was approaching a critical juncture with the Intifada and the peace process. Also, Fateh wanted to hold onto its strong base among the conservative community in the Gaza area and the leftist groups had little support, averaging no more than 3–4 percent of support each.[24] Kuttab summed up the discussions about the Gaza situation with some of the men in the Popular Front leadership this way: We said, "The daughters of Gaza are being harassed daily [by young men claiming to represent Islam]." And the comrades answered, "We don't want a civil war; this is not the time."

In the West Bank the practice of veiling spread everywhere, but was done more voluntarily. For one thing, enforcement would have been rather complicated because of the existence of sizable Christian communities in some of the cities like Jerusalem and Ramallah (and there were thousands of Jewish settlers). The paramount political reason, however, was that the secular nationalist forces were more in control there. And when challenged, they fought back.

It happened in Hebron, a city 35 km south of Jerusalem. Hebron's Arabic name is Khalil, which means "friend," referring to Abraham who is called "friend of God." Hebron is a socially conservative city, better known for its Tomb of Abraham and the February 25, 1994 massacre, when an Israeli settler killed and wounded dozens of Palestinians who were praying at the mosque there. Hebron is less known for the confrontation over the veil that once happened in its streets. In Hebron, some unveiled women from the Palestinian Women's Committees were harassed while walking down a street. In the confrontation that ensued, the women obtained assistance from masked male comrades from the Popular Front, who came to their rescue. Interestingly, the harassers, who were taken away by the masked men and later interrogated, were found to be Arab collaborators with Israeli forces, and not from Hamas. This was not surprising, for it was commonly known in Palestinian political circles that the Israeli intelligence sometimes used collaborators to muddy relations between competing Palestinian groups.[25]

The PLO leadership in the diaspora did not publicly take issue with Hamas's enforcement of the veil in the Gaza Strip, but the Unified Leadership (the Intifada's secret leadership) finally did in August 1989. The Unified Leadership issued its condemnation in communique number 43, after an incident in which two unveiled women activists were attacked. This particular attack was a special affront to the nationalists because the women who were harassed wore the kaffiyeh—the traditional Arab headdress that was symbolic of the Palestinian movement. The communique said: "Nobody has the right to accost women and girls in the streets on the basis of their dress or absence of a veil."[26] A similar statement was issued by the Higher Women's Council, which spoke for the four unions of women's committees.

Neither the diasporan women's leadership nor those in the Occupied Territories perceived the veil issue to be urgent, however. In my interviews during the period 1990–1991, I had asked what each thought of the impact of Islamic fundamentalism on women's participation in public life. The vast majority, regardless of ideological orientation or locale, thought the threat might be serious, but that it was not critical. Even after the veil was imposed in Gaza, the fundamentalist challenge remained decidedly peripheral to the national question.

The women's leadership did not deny that there was a danger of women losing ground to fundamentalism. Several members, however, felt it necessary to point out that Islam is a tolerant religion whose history offered many models of strong women. They uniformly saw fundamentalism as extremist and deviant from Palestinian traditions and the realities of modern society. "I respect that they have their own point of view," one leader said, "but it is not for our times."

Few had anything to say about future strategies to deal with fundamentalism, but hoped that in a Palestinian democracy women would gain political representation, employment rights, and personal status rights. Eisheh Odeh from the Democratic Front's Political Bureau (now with Fida) was keen about the need to communicate with the fundamentalists: "I am interested in opening dialogue with them, listen to them. I am interested in their democratic evolution more than to just stop wearing [the veil]."

Communication with the men in the fundamentalist movement would be very difficult, suggested PLO diplomat Karma Nabulsi, who resides in the United Kingdom. She thought the problem was that women were invisible to the fundamentalists: "They don't see women. They say women are like this and that, but they are not even talking about women." The fundamentalists only saw women as symbols and chips in the power struggle with the secular forces. Consequently, they ascribed values to them that simply were not realistic.

The challenge of the fundamentalists to the secular forces is not going away anytime soon, and the women's leadership, undoubtedly seasoned politicos, knows it must be prepared in the event that a Palestinian state is created. Ashrawi said she thought the work for women's rights, should a state be created, will certainly intensify because, she said:

> I think there are concerns that are unique to women. I don't think all our problems will be solved the moment we have an independent state. I think we will have more challenges and more problems that have to be dealt with. Not within the context of national struggle but an internal struggle to have a really democ-

ratic state with equality, without discrimination and internal oppression.

There is a general belief among the women's leadership in the diaspora that its sisters in the Occupied Territories have done a better job at making sure their contributions are recognized. Ambassador Shahid thinks women have learned from their earlier mistakes. They will be more demanding, she predicted, not like their sisters in the diaspora who played a big role in the national movement but "didn't know how to make demands." She also warned that "if the woman doesn't demand her rights no one is going to give them to her."

The veil affair during the period 1988–1989, however, revealed a critical weakness in the women's leadership: it did not speak with one voice on an issue at the heart of women's privacy and autonomy. Hamas's ability to enforce its will in the Gaza Strip also demonstrated how powerless the women's leadership in fact was. For many, it was a painful reminder that in the Occupied Territories, as in the diaspora, the women's question was captured by the exigencies of national politics.

VII.

It was only after I returned, on subsequent visits, that I realized that, in the winter and spring of 1990, I had stumbled across an already changed landscape of the Women's Committees' Movement. The national question had rechannelled the course of its women's leadership, as it had done to the Women's Union in the diaspora. The pressure from Islamic fundamentalism remained, but also the hard work in the Intifada had taken its toll on the leadership, as the fatigue was plain in the women's faces. But at the heart of the change was the fact that during the period 1988–1990, the peace process was rapidly taking shape, producing a reconfiguration of the Palestinian body politic. The consequences to the women's political agenda proved both complex and detrimental.

In the end, the answer to the question "why did the women's leadership in the Occupied Territories fail to stand up to Hamas in Gaza?" has less to do with its commitment to women's rights and more with how it assessed its political position. Its decision must be seen in the context of the new and unforeseen global and domestic Palestinian developments, which unfolded in the late 1980s. For Kamal and her Women's Action Committees, the issue of the veil could not have arrived at a worse time, for she was at the center of a brewing storm inside the Democratic Front.

For some time, the Democratic Front had heatedly debated Arafat's peace initiative, which was taking the Palestinians on the road to negotiations with Israel. Kamal, who was the leader of the Democratic Front's women's wing in the Occupied Territories, and Yasser Abed Rabbo, out of Tunis, led the group that supported Arafat. Abed Rabbo was the PLO's chief negotiator with the United States at the first official talks, held in Tunis in 1989. The Front's general secretary, Nayef Hawatmeh, was against negotiations until Israel accepted the UN Security Council's resolutions 242 and 338, which meant withdrawing from the 1967 Occupied Territories and addressing the question of the return of the refugees. Unable to reconcile their differences, the two factions went their separate ways in 1991, becoming Democratic Front-Nayef Hawatmeh and Democratic Front-Yasser Abed Rabbo (later the Palestinian Democratic Union Party). The split devastated the Women's Action Committees, the largest and longest-running of the women's committees.

Hawatmeh's supporters were led by Nada Tweir, an unknown young cadre from the Tulkarm area (and perhaps a fourth-generation leader). Tweir took with her about half of the membership and several of the union's facilities, including the Essawiya Copper Works. The leadership of the union (sixty-six out of seventy members of the policymaking higher committee) stayed with Kamal and, for a while, both kept the same name—though it remained more identified with Kamal's group, which is the more visible of the two because of Kamal's stature in the Palestinian movement. By 1994, however, Kamal's group adopted a more decentralized format, called the Women's Action Union.[27]

Apart from the factional issue, the rebellion against Kamal revealed the growing distance between the leadership and the ranks that felt there was an excessive concentration of decision-making at the top. This was recognized by Kamal and her colleagues in the June 1991 and July 1992 reports of the higher committee. It was a symptom of the growing pains that all the women's groups felt after the influx of members during the Intifada. But seen in another light, the challenge from the ranks of the Women's Action Committees showed that Kamal and the others in the leadership actually succeeded in creating an organization in which the members felt sufficiently confident to stand up to the leadership.

Another outcome of the Democratic Front's schism was a lasting rift between Kamal and her friend, society leader Khalil, who was against Arafat's initiative and Kamal's support of it. Khalil was officially unaffiliated with any of the factions, but her views were known to be sympathetic to Hawatmeh's wing and, furthermore, her son, Saji Salameh Khalil, was in that group's Political Bureau. In any case, it is difficult to know all that was involved in their conflict, but Khalil's enmity to Kamal conveys the sense that somehow she felt betrayed.

The crisis in the Women's Action Committees was painful to leaders of the other unions of women's committees, especially when accusations and recriminations were made public in the newspapers. It was, one said, like airing their dirty laundry. The women's leadership knew that for the women's movement to be effective, it must be kept out of factional struggles. This deeply felt sentiment did not alter the reality, however, that first and foremost the members of the women's leadership were daughters of their respective factions.

The other group that suffered from a changing political situation was the Working Women's Committees. Khriesheh's union had a unique problem in that, along with its sponsor, the Palestine Communist party, it had lost its support after the disintegration of the Soviet block in the late 1980s; now the party goes by the name the Palestine People's Party. The communist women's group had few resources to begin with and was in no shape to compete with the services provided by the other PLO women's organizations. By 1992, the effort of the Working Women's Committees to remain a grassroots organization became an uphill battle, and Khriesheh and her colleagues turned to a broader feminist agenda and, for a time, explored merging with fellow feminists in the Women's Action Committees.

The other two unions, the Palestinian Women's Committees and the Social Work Committees, remained largely intact; the latter even benefitted with the infusion of additional funds from its sponsor Fateh, which was expanding its mass base *vis-a-vis* Hamas in the Occupied Territories.

VIII.

Meanwhile, Khalil rejuvenated the West Bank branch of the PLO's Women's Union, which had gone underground in 1966 after being banned by the Jordanian government that controlled the area at that time. Like its parent group, it called itself the General Union of Palestinian Women and was structured as a leadership council of the different Palestinian women's groups, much like the Women's Union secretariat. But unlike the Tunis leadership, it was led by the charitable societies, with all groups equally represented. The twenty-five-member council seated representatives of the charitable societies, the unions of women's committees, and the Society of Women Academics.

The academics were a new element in the coalition of women's nationalist groups and represented those who, for the most part, were previously unorganized but had gained visibility since the Intifada. Their contribution to the Palestinian cause centered on speaking and writing about the social, health, and economic situations of Palestinian women under occupation.

Khalil's council was the culmination of a two-year effort by the Women's Union to create a unified women's front in the Occupied Territories. In 1990, Women's Union President Abdel Hadi thought she had wrenched an agreement from all the sides for what was to be called the Unified Women's Council. The agreement was reached when Abdel Hadi attended a non-governmental organizations meeting, held by the United Nations in Vienna in February 1990.

However, the Unified Women's Council never materialized because the idea did not sit well with anyone in the Occupied Territories' women's leadership. Some in the powerful women's societies of Jerusalem were threatened by a more visible connection to the PLO (that resonated of the earlier debate among the societies in 1965). And, Khalil herself was less than enthusiastic, fearing being outnumbered and out-maneuvered by the women's committees. The women's committees were also reserved about having the academics sit as equals on the leadership council when they had not paid their dues in grassroots organizing. Khalil's council was a different matter, however, because it represented an already existent, though dormant, Women's Union branch, which gave it instant legitimacy.

The council was also a political coup for Khalil, providing a wider national forum beyond her own society, In'ash al-Usra. Khalil's leadership derived from her status as a community leader who accumulated a great deal of goodwill from families that her society assisted—literally for decades. She belongs, however, to the notables class who, after the 1976 municipal elections, uneasily coexisted with the leadership of the PLO-affiliated mass organizations. First-generation Khalil is also approaching her 70s, and so it is difficult to know how she will be able to translate her legacy of community service into political gains.

IX.

Hamas made one more attempt to impose a more conservative attire on the women in Gaza. It was during the Muslim month of fasting, Ramadan, in 1990. In speeches at the mosques and in graffiti, women were urged to wear the *jilbab*, the long black dress mainly worn in the Egyptian country-side and by bedouins. This was the dreaded sequel that Kuttab feared would remove women altogether from political participation in the streets. Putting it simply, Kuttab said: "If [a woman] wears the *jilbab*, she couldn't run away from the soldiers. This is a practical matter." In my visits to Gaza in 1991 and 1993, there were no signs that the long black dress had taken on.[28] But the overall situation of women after the fundamentalist upsurge did not look good.

This was also the consensus at the Bisan conference. The conference, "The Intifada and Some Women's Social Issues," was held in December 1990 in Jerusalem and attended by some 700 people, mostly female politicos. The idea for the meeting came from leaders of the four unions of women's committees who were at first interested in focusing on the veil. The women's studies' committee at Bisan, which organized the conference and had representatives from all the women's unions, decided to broaden the agenda. Its chair, Kuttab, explained that the veil was too sensitive an issue and might have inhibited conference attendance.

Presentations by academics and community activists provided a sobering conclusion. Women had lost out and became politically marginalized after the first few months of the Intifada. The speakers pointed to the emergence of several indicators of a backward movement in the social situation of women, such as the return of early marriages for girls, increased school truancy, and a rise in family violence. At the workshop on the women's committees—which was the most widely attended—there was an underlying realization that grassroots mobilization of women had slowed tremendously.

The consensus of the women's committees' workshop was that there needed to be more attention paid to women's special problems. The time had also come, the women's committees' workshop recommended, to begin drafting a personal status law in a future Palestinian state.[29] Kuttab explained that the Intifada helped the women's leadership understand the depth of the social issue—not just believe it in theory. The workshop also reflected the phenomenon that movement of the national question to the diplomatic level and the decline in mobilizational work made it possible for the women's leadership in the Occupied Territories to focus more on its common interests in women's rights and issues.

Because of the agreements reached between Israel and the PLO in Oslo, Washington, and Cairo during the period 1993–1994 (and as of this writing are still ongoing), the women's leadership entered a new stage in the national liberation struggle, in which Palestinians began to administer some of their own affairs in the West Bank and Gaza Strip. The first breakthrough between the PLO and Israel was the Declaration of Principles of September 13, 1993, which drew up a blueprint for a transitional stage of self-rule, to be followed in five years by a final settlement of the status of the 1967 occupied areas as well as for a resolution of all outstanding issues. For the Palestinians, control of the West Bank, Gaza Strip and East Jerusalem, and solving the problem of the refugees, were crucial elements of a true compromise and peace between the two peoples. Arafat and his supporters (Fateh, the Palestinian Democratic Union Party, formerly Yasser Abed Rabbo's splinter of the Democratic Front, and the Palestine

People's Party, formerly the communists) thought that negotiations would eventually produce this outcome. Those in opposition, led by the Popular Front and the Democratic Front, had little hope during the negotiations, arguing that Arafat had followed undemocratic procedures and had drastically deviated from the Palestinian consensus regarding how to achieve a Palestinian state. These disagreements were vehemently argued in private and public forums, including women's circles, but Arafat's side continued to prevail.

The transitional stage began in mid-May, 1994, when the PLO took charge of some 60 percent of the Gaza Strip, and a few kilometers in and around Jericho in the West Bank, as spelled out in the Cairo Agreement of May 4, 1994. The new administration for the transitional stage was the Palestinian National Authority, a body of diasporan and local Palestinian ministers who were appointed and headed by Arafat (who had moved to Gaza in July 1994). Most of the PLO offices in Tunis were then closed, leaving mainly the Political and the National Affairs departments, which dealt with foreign and Arab affairs that are outside the framework of the Israeli-Palestinian agreement.

Two women received high-level appointments in the Palestinian National Authority: Um Jihad became Minister of Social Affairs, and Bernawi became head of the women's contingent of the Palestinian Police. Also, Kamal, who was a founding leader of the women's movement in the Occupied Territories in the 1980s, expects to head a Women's Affairs Council in the Palestinian National Authority. The Council, which received the initial go-ahead from Arafat, was officially proposed by Kamal on November 17, 1994. If created, it will be attached to Arafat's office, with the purpose of advising and making recommendations to the president, and the various ministries about women's issues. The Council will also be responsible for data collection, research, and planning functions. In contrast, Ashrawi, who led in the peace process, thus far has opted not to participate in the Palestinian National Authority. Turning her attention to human rights issues, she established and now directs the Independent Palestinian Commission for Citizen Rights, headquartered in Jerusalem.

X.

On August 3, 1994, the women's leadership in the West Bank held a press conference at the National Hotel in East Jerusalem and presented a proposal on women's rights called "Draft Document of Principles of Women's Rights," also known as the Women's Charter. It is a three-page document that called attention to women's lengthy participation in the liberation struggle and the need to address women's concerns in the new stage of state formation.

The Women's Charter enumerated women's various contributions and sacrifices and called for action, saying:

> The Palestinian women's struggle has been depicted over the decades of the Palestinian national struggle as an immeasurable contribution in all spheres; women were martyred and thousands imprisoned. Palestinian women also played a vital role in the preservation of the unity of the Palestinian family as a social base to support individuals in the absence of a Palestinian national authority. Palestinian women were forced to delay many tasks associated with their social position and instead focus all their attention towards the issues of the national and political struggle. It is time that the issue of women's legal rights in all aspects become a cornerstone for building a democratic Palestinian society.

The Charter called for equality in political, civil, economic, social, and cultural rights and for incorporating a "document of principles on women's legal status into the constitution and the legislation of the future Palestinian state." The message of the women's representatives was pointed: The Palestinian woman had "proven herself" and now expected equal rights.

The Women's Charter was presented under the name of the General Union of Palestinian Women. The initiative had come from the West Bank leadership in the spring, when it called upon the Women's Union secretariat to draw up a draft document. This it did. Afterwards, the paper was circulated for review, first among the women's committees and then the charitable societies. All the groups backed the initiative; the meeting at the National Hotel was the first occasion where it was presented to the general public.

Almost the entire top leadership of women's societies and women's committees sat at the head table at the press conference: Khalil of Ina'sh al-Usra, representing the West Bank branch of the Women's Union and also the Union of Voluntary Women's Societies; Khriesheh of the Working Women's Committees of the Palestine People's Party; Diab of the Social Work Committees of Fateh; Kuttab of the Palestinian Women's Committees of the Popular Front (however, the head of the group, Nassar, was absent); and Siham Barghouti, who, since 1993, has headed the Women's Action Union of the Palestinian Democratic Union Party. Kamal, also present, had stepped down from leading her group in 1992 to focus on matters relating to the Palestinian National Authority.[30]

Two women from the diasporan women's leadership were also at the head table: Mayada Bamia Abbas, from the secretariat of the Women's Union (she and her family had a one-month permit to visit Jerusalem), and Um Jihad, who had come with Arafat in July to live in her hometown of Gaza. She had been given Israeli permission to make visits to the West Bank and Jerusalem. Um Jihad attended the press conference to lend her support to the Women's Charter, in her capacity as Minister of Social Affairs in the Palestinian National Authority. Both Um Jihad and Suha, wife of Arafat, have talked about women's rights to the press on several occasions since they have been in Gaza.

The press conference was meant to show the unity of the Palestinian women's organizations behind a women's rights agenda. The conference room was overflowing with veiled and unveiled women who quietly listened as the document was read in Arabic and English. But all did not go smoothly, as chanting and loud protests came from the Popular and Democratic Front activists, who objected to the seating of Um Jihad at the headtable, representing the Palestinian National Authority, which they opposed.[31] The interruption came from women who supported the Charter and not from supporters of the Islamist cause, who remained silent. When the meeting concluded, a somber mood prevailed, as both the crowd and the leadership became resigned to the fact that the forces, which would have to fight for women's rights, were themselves not in full harmony.

There is another important concern in the minds of leadership members, who have been observing the setting up of new professional, labor, and town councils in many localities in recent months. The concern was that there is a serious neglect in the nominations and appointments of women. In one West Bank city, a female lawyer elected to head the local lawyer's committee was reportedly initially ignored by her committee members. The lack of a firm commitment to include women was also evident at the highest levels of decision-making. The technical committees set up by Arafat in late 1993, as temporary predecessors to the Palestinian National Authority (for health, social affairs, etc.), contained no more than 2 percent women. In the Palestinian National Authority, only two women so far, Um Jihad and Bernawi, hold high posts. The conclusion reached at the Bisan Conference in 1990 was that the participation of women in the Intifada had declined, and there was serious concern about what their lowered visibility might mean. The early stages of setting up self-rule confirmed that undoubtedly a deep tradition of sexism still prevails among the comrades in the national struggle, as evidenced by their initial appointments.

For the secularists, the most disheartening discovery was the absence of a political and social environment that could support a secular personal status law that would provide equality to men and women in matters of marriage, divorce, custody, and inheritance. In Islamic law, women are given rights, such as the ability to own property, but there is a definite slant favoring male patronage and guardianship. According to the extensive survey done by the Norwegian organization Fagbevegelsens Senter for Forskning (FAFO) in 1993, the public in the West Bank and Gaza Strip, by a vast margin, supported maintaining the sectarian base of personal status law. The data reveal that no doubt the vast majority of Palestinians see themselves as religiously observant; they favor the veil and an Islamic Palestinian state (versus a secular democratic one). Still, the questionnaire did not address all the important personal status issues, and little is really known about how the people envision the details of an Islamic-oriented state. Interestingly, women tended to be somewhat more likely to support secularism than men (29 percent versus 20 percent), and men were twice as likely to be religious activists than were women (24 percent versus 12 percent).[32] The message from the FAFO survey is that the Palestinian society has not escaped the region-wide Islamic resurgence, which spells an uphill battle for the secularists, whether male or female.

In principle, many in the women's leadership stood for the idea of a secular personal status law. Their Charter called for "full equality regarding issues pertaining to personal status." They were, however, cognizant of the strong social traditions, shown in the FAFO data, and were also aware of the need of the nationalist forces to deal with Hamas and Islamic Jihad in order to entice them to work within the framework of the Palestinian National Authority.

This was made clear to the women's delegation, who in 1994, visited the chair of the jurist committee charged with drafting the Palestinian Basic Law. The Draft Basic Law (April 1994) guaranteed in Article 10 that, "Women and men shall have equal fundamental rights and freedoms without any discrimination and shall be equal before the law." Also, throughout the document the gender-neutral term "person" is used in its proclamation of rights and obligations. The women's delegation had asked the committee chair to do more and commit to a secular personal status law, but his response was that they themselves must wage the political battle for women's rights. In private conversations, several of the women leaders indicated their resignation to the reality founded on the ground that the battle for a secular personal status law was premature. Instead, attentions have turned to more immediate steps, namely educational workshops to educate women about their political and legal rights.

Literally dozens of training workshops and conferences were held in many West Bank and Gaza Strip cities during the period 1993–1994 and were attended by hundreds. The women's workshops focused on elections (expected in 1996), leadership training, and women's rights under Islamic law which, in the West Bank, is the Jordanian law and in the Gaza Strip, the Egyptian law. The protection awarded to women under Islamic law is oftentimes unknown and unpracticed in society at large. For example, a female lawyer at one of these workshops said that approximately 80 percent of the time, inheritances, which are supposed to be divided (though unequally) between sons and daughters, went entirely to the males in the family.

These educational activities tended to be jointly sponsored by the different women's committees. But also participating, and even leading in the effort, were non-partisan, human rights and women's rights centers—especially the al-Haq human rights organization, based in Ramallah, and the Feminist Studies Center and the Women's Law and Social Counseling Center, both in Jerusalem. Funding for these efforts came from international donors, including the United Nations Development Programme and the United States Agency for International Development. The donors required that these projects be non-partisan, serving the entire women's community, and that has helped cement cooperation among the different groups. Officially, however, the women's groups affiliated with the Popular and the Democratic Fronts, being against the Palestinian-Israeli rapprochement, have tended not to participate. No doubt, however, the meagerness of funds available to Palestinian political parties reinforced the women's willingness to pool their resources—something that could change if the parties become richer and better able to support their own women's programs.

By the mid-1990s, the future of the second- and third-generation female leadership was still uncertain. Members were neither optimistic nor pessimistic about developments in the negotiations and the transitional stage, but most were hopeful. They have become more open to cooperation among themselves, and are intent on pursuing a more vigorous women's rights' agenda. The women's leadership in the West Bank and Gaza Strip seem determined to remain at the forefront of the struggle for Palestinian statehood and women's liberation—as they were when they led the Women's Committees' Movement.

EPILOGUE

On the last day of April 1993, Issam Abdel Hadi, head of the PLO Women's Union since its inception, returned home to Nablus from an exile of twenty-four years. She was one of the first group of Palestinians, composed of thirty individuals and their families, that Israel let return as a measure of confidence-building between the two peoples. Her trip from Amman through the Allenby Bridge crossing was highly emotional, with hundreds of well-wishers lining both sides of the border. President of the Families of the Martyrs foundation, Um Jihad, who about a year later would make the same trek, was among those waving farewell. Abdel Hadi stayed in the West Bank for a short while, then returned to Amman to resume her responsibilities at the Women's Union.

A few months later, in November 1993, another member of the diaspora leadership, Salwa Abu Khadra, general secretary of the Women's Union and a leading member of Fateh, travelled from Tunis to visit her homeland as part of a UNESCO delegation. She toured both the Occupied Territories and inside Israel, where she had grown up and had not been able to enter since fleeing in 1948. It was a bittersweet return that gave her hope that she might soon be able to live on Palestinian land again.

Such emotional moments have been experienced by several in the diasporan women's leadership who were able to return to either live in the Palestinian-administered areas or to merely visit those in Israel. The vast majority of the 1948 and 1967 Palestinian refugees have been unable to return to their homeland and, as of this writing, negotiations regarding this issue have not been scheduled. Of the estimated 6,692,153 Palestinian population (1995), close to four million live in the diaspora, 3,437,021 live in Arab countries and another 500,000 live in the rest of the world.[1] About 15 percent of the Palestinians still reside in refugee camps. The future of the refugees of 1948 and 1967 is a critical issue that must be resolved in the final settlement after the five-year transitional period.

The history of the Palestinian women's leadership is about definitive moments. For Abdel Hadi, it might have been the hours spent with the Israeli interrogators in 1969, and the torture of her daughter, which she could never forgive. For Um Jihad, Um Nasser, and Um Lutuf, it might have been the conversations with their husbands, who helped them become pioneers in the Palestinian National Movement. For others, the moments came early in adolescence, such as when Eisheh Odeh discovered she must stand up for her right to an education, regardless of her class, or when Kamal experienced the death of a fellow student, Raja-e Abu Ammasha, who was martyred while trying to take down the British flag from the top of the British consulate in East Jerusalem.

The history of the Palestinian women's leadership is also about experience and memory. The women in the first generation of leaders, like Khalil and Abdel Hadi, were burdened by a sense of defeat and an inability to stand up to Israeli power, which angered them and made them greatly suspicious of the peace process. This sentiment was not unlike that of a large segment of the population in the early '90s, which caused many to adopt a wait-and-see stance toward the implementation potential of the Israeli-PLO accords.

The second and third generations constitute the vast majority of the thirty-four leaders interviewed for this book. They led the greatest grassroots mobilization in the history of the Palestinian woman. It empowered them and taught them many lessons, including how slippery and transient political success could be. The leadership from these generations was divided over the course of the PLO, and the division was mainly along party lines. For example, those in Fateh supported the negotiations with Israel, while those in the Popular Front opposed them. Such disagreements simmered even inside each of the PLO factions, boiling over in the case of the Democratic Front and dividing the largest women's organization in the Occupied Territories. Indeed, every time these eruptions occurred, partisan conflicts took a heavy toll on the women's leadership and its work.

By the mid-1990s, important and interconnected developments provided new challenges for the women's leadership. The major development was the launching of self-government by the Palestinians in the West Bank and Gaza Strip. In addition to the Israeli withdrawal from parts of Gaza and Jericho, several agreements and protocols were signed in 1994 by the Israelis and the Palestinians, which extended self-rule to a number of policy domains (education, health, social welfare, tourism, and taxation) for the Arab population in the remaining parts of the Occupied Territories.

The accompanying development is the shifting of donor countries' support of Palestinian social, educational, and health projects to the new Palestinian public institutions. This means that many of the women's social welfare organizations, which previously relied on donors from abroad, are rapidly becoming marginalized in the allocation of donor funds.

It also means that the women's leadership has to draw up new strategies, which entails working both within the governmental and non-governmental spheres. For examples, Um Jihad's Families of the Martyrs foundation became part of her Social Affairs Ministry; some of the educational programs of women's societies must come under the Education Ministry, and the rehabilitation programs of certain charitable societies will have to be turned over to the Health Ministry. On the other hand, some of the women's charitable societies have considered taking on income-generating projects. For example, the Ina'sh al-Usra charitable society received funds from one of the ruling princes in the United Arab Emirates to build a frozen food factory at their main site in al-Bireh. In the end, everyone recognizes that there is always a need for charitable work in the Palestinian society, as in all others. The women's societies are old and established institutions of Palestinian civil society, and are guaranteed to be active participants in softening the sharp edges of the transition from occupation to self-rule. The future of the women's committees, however, is not so clear.

The women's committees, which were always more openly political and partisan, have now turned to more direct political education tasks such as workshops on elections and personal status law. Generally, however, they are abandoning kindergartens and other social services to the Palestinian administration and to the women's charitable societies, including those in the Islamic camp that have become much better funded. Turning to women's political education and other feminist interests is by no means saying that the women's leadership is subordinating its lifelong nationalist interests to "gender interests," in the words of Molyneux.[2] The interplay between the two interests, however, has begun to be more openly addressed, and how each group and leader will face the women's rights challenge during the state-forming stage will be revealed in the coming years.

A few of the members of the women's leadership have gone into effective retirement, such as Um Nasser, who headed Arafat's office in the early years, and Laila Khaled, who moved with her family to Amman in 1993 and is preoccupied, for the moment, with raising her two children. Some like Abla Abu Elbi and Samira Abu Ghazaleh should continue to serve the large Palestinian refugee community in the diaspora. Others from the diaspora leadership, Nihaya Muhammad, Shadia Helou, Sulafa Hijawi, Fatima Bernawi, and Vera Naufal, returned to the West Bank and Gaza Strip—and others are on their way there. As of this writing, however, almost all in the women's leadership—those leading in their respective political parties, in the women's organizations, and in the PLO offices in the diaspora—are poised to play key roles in setting the agenda for the new nation. They have the advantage of all the lessons of the national liberation struggle, and have a great responsibility to convey those lessons to the upcoming fourth generation of leaders.

The women's leadership has participated in all the periods of the Palestinian National Movement in Amman, Beirut, Tunis, and East Jerusalem. They were there during moments of superb accomplishment and also moments of great devastation. There is no question that, as an institutional component of the Palestinian nationalist movement, the women's leadership has gained in strength and stature; indeed, the women have "proven themselves." How they will reap the benefits in terms of participating in the lawmaking process for the West Bank and Gaza Strip remains to be seen. Meanwhile, the circle that began with the first generation will be completed when the leadership returns to Jerusalem. As I write, the familiar diehards are blending with fresh faces. And traces of those who came before, although sometimes forgotten, somehow always remain in a hidden dance with the new.

APPENDIX: INTERVIEW LIST

In Alphabetical Order:

Abdel Hadi, In'am. Fateh. Member of the Palestinian Lawyers Union secretariat and the Palestine National Council. Interview held in 1990 in Amman, Jordan.

Abdel Hadi, Issam. Independent. President of the General Union of Palestinian Women and member of the Palestine National Council and its Central Council. Interviews held in 1990 and 1991 in Amman, Jordan, and on subsequent occasions by telephone from the United States.

Abdel Rahim, Wedad. Arab Liberation Front. Member of the General Union of Palestinian Women secretariat, the Palestine National Council, and its Central Council. She is the wife of now-deceased general secretary of the Arab Liberation Front, Ahmad Abdel Rahim, thus is head of the women's office in that faction. Interview held in 1990 in Amman, Jordan.

Abu Ali, Khadijeh. Fateh. Member of the General Union of Palestinian Women secretariat, Fateh's Revolutionary Council, and the Palestine National Council. Interviews held in 1990 in Amman, Jordan, and in Tunis, Tunisia, and subsequently, by telephone.

Abu Elbi, Abla. Democratic Front for the Liberation of Palestine. Member of the General Union of Palestinian Women secretariat, the Democratic Front's Central Committee, and the Palestine National Council. Interviews held in 1990 and 1991 in Amman, Jordan.

Abu Ghazaleh, Samira. Independent. Head of the General Union of Palestinian Women branch in Egypt (the Palestinian Women's League) and member of the Palestine National Council. Interview held in 1990 in Cairo, Egypt.

133

Abu Khadra, Salwa. Fateh. General-secretary of the General Union of Palestinian Women and member of Fateh's Revolutionary Council, the Palestine National Council, and its Central Council. Interviewed in 1990 in Tunis, Tunisia.

Ashrawi, Hanan. Independent. Former spokesperson for the Palestinian delegation to the Middle East Peace Conference. In 1993, she turned her attentions to human rights issues and is now director of the Independent Commission for Citizen Rights, which she founded. Interview held in 1990 in Ramallah, West Bank.

al-Atrash, Maryam. Fateh. Member of the General Union of Palestinian Women secretariat, Fateh's Revolutionary Council, and the Palestine National Council. Interview held in 1990 in Tunis, Tunisia.

Bernawi, Fatima. Fateh. Highest female in Fateh militia with the rank of major, member of Fateh's Revolutionary Council, and the Palestine National Council. She now heads the women's police in the Palestinian National Authority. Interview held in 1990 in Tunis, Tunisia.

Diab, Rabiha. Fateh. Highest ranking woman in Fateh in the Occupied Territories and president of Fateh's Union of Social Work Committees. Interviews held in 1990 and 1991 in Ramallah, West Bank.

Helou, Jihan. Fateh. Former member of the General Union of Palestinian Women secretariat (1974–1985) and the Palestine National Council. She is an early member of Fateh in Lebanon. Interviews held in 1990 and 1991 in London, the United Kingdom, and on subsequent occasions, by telephone.

Helou, Shadia. Fateh. Former head of the General Union of Palestinian Women branch in Lebanon (1974–1982) and member of the Palestine National Council. After leaving Lebanon, she worked as a writer at Fateh's Tunis headquarters. Interview held in 1990 in Tunis, Tunisia.

Hijawi, Sulafa. Fateh. Advisor to Yasser Arafat, she worked out of his office in Tunis and is a member of the Palestine National Council. Interview held in 1990 in Tunis, Tunisia.

Kamal, Zahira. Democratic Front for the Liberation of Palestine. She was the front's highest ranking woman in the Occupied Territories, a member of its Political Bureau, and president of its Union of Women's Action Committees (until 1992). After the Front split into two, Kamal went with the Palestinian Democratic Union Party, formed by her and Yasser Abed Rabbo, and is a member of the party's Executive Committee. She is expected to hold the portfolio of Women's Affairs in the Palestinian

National Authority. Interviews held in 1990, 1991, 1993, and 1994 in Jerusalem and Tunis, and on other occasions, by telephone.

Khaled, Laila. Popular Front for the Liberation of Palestine. President of the Front's women's organization and member of the Palestine National Council. Interviews held in 1990 in Damascus, Syria, and on subsequent occasions, by telephone from the United States.

Khalil, Samiha (also known as Um Khalil). Independent. Community leader and president of In'ash Al-Usra Society, located in al-Bireh, West Bank. Interviews held in 1990 and 1994 in al-Bireh and, on other occasions, by telephone.

Khriesheh, Amal. Palestine Communist Party (now the Palestinian People's Party). President of the Union of Working Women's Committees affiliated with that party. Interviews held in 1990 and 1993 in Ramallah and Jerusalem.

Kuttab, Eileen. Popular Front for the Liberation of Palestine. Former head of the development program of the Front's Union of Palestinian Women's Committees. Since 1990, she has been head of the women's studies committee at Bisan Center, a political research institution, and also helped establish the women's studies program at Birzeit University. Interviews held in 1990 in New York, the United States, in 1994 in the West Bank, and, on other occasions, by telephone.

Muhammad, Nihaya. Democratic Front for the Liberation of Palestine. Member of the General Union of Palestinian Women secretariat, the Front's Central Committee, and the Palestine National Council. Interview held in 1990 in Damascus, Syria.

Mustafa, Salwa. Fateh. High ranking officer in the PLO National Relations Department. Interview held in 1990 in Tunis, Tunisia.

Nassar, Maha. Popular Front for the Liberation of Palestine. President of the Front's Union of Palestinian Women's Committees. Interview held in 1990 in Ramallah, West Bank.

Naufal, Vera. Democratic Front for the Liberation of Palestine (now with the Palestinian Democratic Union Party). High ranking officer in the PLO National Relations Department and a member of the Palestine National Council. Interview held in 1990 in Tunis, Tunisia.

Odeh, Eisheh. Democratic Front for the Liberation of Palestine (now with the Palestinian Democratic Union Party). Member of the Democratic Front's Political Bureau and now in the Palestinian Democratic Union's Executive Committee. She is also a member of the Palestine National

Council. Interviews held in 1991 in Amman, Jordan, and, on other occasions, by telephone from the United States.

Odeh, Rasmiyeh. Popular Front for the Liberation of Palestine. Member of the Front's Central Committee and the Palestine National Council. Interview held in 1990 in Amman, Jordan.

Sayigh, Mai. Fateh. Former general-secretary of the General Union of Palestinian Women (1974–1985) and former member of Fateh's Revolutionary Council and the Palestine National Council. Interviewed by mail in 1990 and, on subsequent occasions, by telephone.

Shahid, Laila. Fateh. PLO ambassador to France and member of Fateh. Interview held in 1990 in Tunis, Tunisia.

Sha'ath, Maisoun. Fateh. Member of the General Union of Palestinian Women secretariat and the Palestine National Council. Interview held in 1990 in Cairo, Egypt.

Um Jihad (Intissar al-Wazir). Fateh. President of the PLO Families of the Martyrs foundation, member of Fateh Central Committee, the Palestine National Council, and now minister of Social Affairs in the Palestinian National Authority. Interviews held in 1990 and 1991 in Amman, Jordan, and, on other occasions, by telephone from the United States.

Um Lutuf (Nabila al-Nemer). Fateh. Member of Fateh's Revolutionary Council and the Palestine National Council. Interview held in 1990 in Tunis, Tunisia.

Um Manhal (Lucia Hijazi). Fateh. President of the General Union of Palestinian Women Administrative Council and the Palestine National Council. Interview held in 1990 in Amman, Jordan.

Um Nasser (Najla Yassin). Fateh. Member of the General Union of Palestinian Women secretariat, Fateh's Revolutionary Council and the Palestine National Council. She is the former head of PLO chairman Yasser Arafat's office. Interview held in 1990 in Tunis, Tunisia.

Um Sabri (Jamila Saidam). Fateh. Member of the General Union of Palestinian Women secretariat, Fateh's Revolutionary Council, and the Palestine National Council. Interview held in 1990 in Tunis, Tunisia.

Yousuf, Faiza. Independent. Member of the General Union of Palestinian Women secretariat, initially for the Palestine Liberation Front, but since the mid-'80s has been an independent and member of the Palestine National Council. Interview held in 1990 in Tunis, Tunisia.

Other Leaders and Activists:

Abdel Rahim, Ahmad. At the time of the interview, he was head of the PLO Department of Mass Organizations (he died in 1991). Interview held in 1990 in Amman, Jordan.

Arid, Najat. Fateh organizer in Lebanon in the 1970s. At the time of the interview, she was section head in the PLO's Department of Social Affairs. Interview held in 1990 in Tunis, Tunisia.

Bernawi, Ihsan. Member of the Palestine National Council for Fateh and worked in the Social Services Committee of the Families of the Martyrs foundation. She is the sister of Fatima Bernawi and a former guerrilla fighter. Interview held in 1990 in Amman, Jordan.

Eid, Suha. Head of the office of Birzeit University Extension in Amman, Jordan, and a member of Fateh. Interview held in 1990 in Amman, Jordan.

Fatima. An organizer in the West Bank for the Union of Women's Action Committees. Interview held in 1990 in Cairo, Egypt.

Jamila. An organizer in the Gaza Strip for the Union of Women's Action Committees. Interview held in 1990 in Cairo, Egypt.

Melhem, Muhammad. At the time of the interview, he was head of the PLO Department of the Affairs of the Occupied Homeland. Interview held in 1990 in Amman, Jordan.

Mulhis, Ghania. Member of the administrative committee of the Children of Martyrs Works Society (acronym Samed) in the 1970s. She later worked as an economist at the Tunis headquarters of the Arab League of Nations. Interview held in 1990 in Tunis, Tunisia.

Nabulsi, Karma. At the time of the interview, she was second in command at the PLO office in London and is a member of Fateh. Interview held in 1990 in London, United Kingdom.

Odeh, Rouda. An organizer in the West Bank for the Union of Palestinian Women Committees. Interviewed in 1990 in Cairo, Egypt.

Sa'ad, Alice. Member of Union of Women's Charity Societies in the West Bank. Interview held in 1990 in Cairo, Egypt.

Sayeh, Abdel Hamid (title Shaykh). At the time of the interview, he was president of the Palestine National Council. Interview held in 1990 in Amman, Jordan.

Sha'ath, Nabil. Senior advisor to Yasser Arafat and head of the Palestine National Council's Political Committee. He is also a member of the Fateh Central Committee and the chief negotiator in the Palestinian-Israeli talks. Interview held in 1990 in Cairo, Egypt.

Siyam, Hana. Member of the General Union of Palestinian Women Administrative Council for Fateh. Interview held in 1990 in Amman, Jordan.

Nassar Tarazi, Rima. Member of Ina'sh al-Usra Society in Bireh, West Bank, and an independent. Interview held in 1990 in Amman, Jordan.

NOTES

PROLOGUE

1. The Occupied Territories refer to the West Bank, Gaza Strip, and East Jerusalem. These are the central and southwestern regions of Palestine which, under the 1949 armistice agreements between the newly formed state of Israel and the neighboring Arab states, came under the administration of Jordan (West Bank and East Jerusalem) and Egypt (Gaza Strip). In the 1967 War, these areas, along with the Sinai in Egypt and the Golan Heights in Syria, were occupied by Israel. The Camp David Agreement of 1978, the peace accord between Egypt and Israel, returned the Sinai to Egypt. In 1994, part of the Gaza Strip and the Jericho area in the West Bank were given self-rule as part of the transitional stage of the Palestinian-Israeli accords of 1993–1994.

2. Sometimes, those without a son also receive this title from their friends and relatives out of respect. For example, Yasser Arafat, who had no children, was called Abu Ammar.

CHAPTER 1. THREE GENERATIONS OF WOMEN LEADERS

1. The terms "revolution," "armed struggle" and "resistance" were popularly used in the early days of the Palestinian National Movement (late '60s–'70s), but since the growth of PLO institutions in the late '70s, the term "liberation organization" is more prevalent.

2. Laila Jammal, *Contributions by Palestinian Women to the National Struggle for Liberation* (Washington, D.C.: Middle East Public Relations, 1985), p.12.

3. For a well-documented review of these European policies, see David Fromkin, *A Peace to End All Peace* (New York: Henry Holt and Co., 1989).

4. The earliest and most authoritative account of the 1920s and 1930s Arab women's movement in Palestine is Matiel Mogannam's *The Arab Woman and the Palestinian Problem* (Westport: Hyperion Press, Inc., 1976 reprint of 1937 Arabic version). Mogannam, who lived her latter years in the Washington, D.C. area, had participated in the march on the office of the British High Commissioner and in the First Arab Women's Congress.

5. See, for example, the biographical account of Mary Shehadeh in Orayb Najjar's, *Portraits of Palestinian Women* (Salt Lake City, University of Utah Press, 1992).

6. See Rosemary Sayigh, *Palestinians: From Peasants to Revolutionaries* (London: Zed Books Ltd., 1979).

7. Nasser H. Aruri and Samih Farsoun, "Palestinian Communities and Arab Host Countries," in *The Sociology of the Palestinians*, edited by Khalil Nakhleh and Elia Zureik (New York: St. Martin's Press, 1980), pp.112–146.

8. Fawaz Turki, *The Disinherited* (New York: Monthly Review Press, 1972), p.91.

9. The period of the 1920s–1940s witnessed the rise of several Arab states: the Kingdom of Saudi Arabia and the Hashemite Kingdom of Iraq in 1932, the Republic of Syria in 1946, and the Republic of Lebanon in 1943. Syria has since witnessed several military coups. The Egyptian monarchy gained nominal independence from the British in 1922 and was later toppled during the 1952 Revolution, which drove the British out and abolished the monarchy; the Iraqi monarchy was destroyed in the 1958 Revolution.

10. See Avi Shlaim, "The Rise and Fall of the All-Palestine Government in Gaza," *Journal of Palestine Studies* 20 (Autumn 1990): pp. 37–53.

11. This is based on a survey using the subject index for 1952–1965 in Gamal Abdel-Nasser's, *Collection of Speeches, Announcements, and Declarations of the President* (Cairo: UAR Information Service, July 23, 1952–June, 1964), subject index in ibid., vols. I–IV. (Arabic).

12. James Jankowski, "Egyptian Responses to the Palestine Problem in the Interwar Period," *International Journal of Middle Eastern Studies*, 12(1980): pp. 1–38.

13. Nasser, *Collection of Speeches, Announcements, and Declarations of the President*, vol. II.

14. Alan Hart noted a similar conversation in 1959 in which Abu Jihad warned his future wife Intissar al-Wazir (Um Jihad) of the dangers

awaiting. See Hart's *Arafat: A Political Biography* (Bloomington: Indiana University Press, 1984), p. 135.

15. Khadijeh Abu Ali, *Introduction to Women's Reality and their Experience in the Palestinian Revolution* (Beirut: General Union of Palestinian Women, 1975). (Arabic).

16. An English language source about the objectives and strategies of the Palestinian armed struggle is Hisham Sharabi's, *Palestine Guerrillas*, Monographs Series, No. 25 (Beirut: The Institute for Palestine Studies, 1970). Early Fateh thought can be found in its magazine *al-Thawra-al-Filastiniya* (The Palestinian Revolution) and the Popular Front's in its *al-Hadaf* (The Purpose). The ideas of various Palestinian factions can be found in Arabic in booklet-size mimeographs. In regard to communist literature, often cited is *Mao Tse-tung's Selected Writings* (Beijing: Foreign Languages Press, 1961 and 1965). Also cited is General Yu Nguyen Giap's, *The People's War and the People's Army* (Hanoi: Foreign Languages Press, 1961). Reference to Ernesto Che-Guevara did not focus on any particular part of his writing; the volume most likely to have become accessible to the Palestinian revolutionaries in 1968 is his *Guerrilla de Guerrillas in Obra Revolucianaria* (Mexico: Ediciones Era Mexico, D.F., 1967).

17. Statistics on the Palestinian population are generally estimates because, other than refugee camp residents, no Palestinian-specific statistics are usually collected and Palestinians are dispersed throughout the Arab world. For education rates, see Yvonne Haddad, "Palestinian Women: Patterns of Legitimation and Domination," in *The Sociology of the Palestinians*, pp.147–175. See also, George Kossaifi's, "Demographic Characteristics of the Arab Palestinian People," in the same publication, pp.13–46.

18. For references to honor in Arab culture, see Elizabeth Warnock Fernea, ed., *Women and the Family in the Middle East* (Austin: University of Texas Press, 1985); Nahid Toubia, ed., *Women of the Arab World* (London: Zed Books Ltd., 1988); Fatima Mernissi, *Beyond the Veil*, revised edition (Bloomington, Ind. Indiana University Press, 1987); and Margot Badran and Miriam Cooke, eds., *Opening the Gates* (Bloomington: Indiana University Press, 1990).

19. In a 1975 study, Ghazi Khalili examined the progress of women in the Palestinian movement in Lebanon and found that women in the militia camps and those working in the PLO office heard that sometimes fellow male comrades thought of them as sexually available, in Ghazi Khalili's, *Palestinian Women and the Revolution* (Beirut: Palestine Liberation Organization Research Center, 1977) (Arabic). When peace negotiator Ashrawi, who lives in the West Bank, was part of the Palestinian negotiating team following the Madrid Peace Conference, she also was subjected

to sexual innuendo in a circular by the Popular Front, which opposed the peace talks.

20. Not all the PLO factions showed genuine interest in recruiting women. Some, like al-Saiqa and the Popular Front for the Liberation of Palestine-General Command (a splinter of the Popular Front), were essentially bands of militias affiliated with Syria. Others with longer histories of popular mobilization—Fateh, the Popular Front, the Democratic Front, and the Palestine Communist Party—had active women's frameworks. The women's office of the Iraqi-supported Arab Liberation Front was active mainly in the latter part of the 1970s in Lebanon.

21. For her life history, see Leila Khaled's, *My People Shall Live: The Autobiography of a Revolutionary*, edited by George Hajjar (London: Hodder and Stoughton, 1973).

22. A translation of the poem can be found in Fernea, *Women and the Family in the Middle East*, p.168.

CHAPTER 2. AMMAN: EARLY YEARS OF REVOLUTIONARY STRUGGLE

1. The PLO's Executive Committee was headed by the lawyer Ahmad Shukayri, who worked previously as a diplomat for Saudi Arabia.

2. My translation from the text, in Khalili's, *Palestinian Women and the Revolution*, p.105.

3. For a brief record of Palestinian women's political involvement during the unrest of the 1920s through the early 1980s, see Jammal, *Contributions of Palestinian Women to the National Struggle for Liberation*.

4. This account is from Soraya Antonius', "Prisoners for Palestine: A List of Women Political Prisoners," *Journal of Palestine Studies*, 9, 3(1980): pp.29–80.

5. Other leaders of women's societies who attended the congresses of 1964–65 and who remained under Israeli occupation, like Samiha Khalil of In'ash al-Usra and Yusra Barbari of the Palestine Women's Union of Gaza, maintained a politically low profile for much of the time while dedicating their lives to charitable work.

6. Sharabi, *Palestine Guerrillas: Their Credibility and Effectiveness*, pp.55–61.

7. In its Political Report dated August 1967, the Popular Front talked about the interconnectedness of the Palestinian question and Arab politics, and that the "Palestinian resistance movement should judge Arab conditions according to their tangible positions toward the Palestinian question. . . ."

8. Abu Iyad, (nom de guerre of Salah Khalaf, with Eric Rouleau), *My Home, My Land: A Narrative of the Palestinian Struggle* (New York: Times Books, 1981), pp.55–56.

9. The first female was Shadia Abu Ghazaleh, who was killed in 1969.

10. Khalili, *Palestinian Women and the Revolution,* throughout.

11. Kamel Mansi, "The Palestinian Refugee Camps in Jordan," *Samed al-Iqtisadi* 13, 83 (January/February/March, 1991): pp.79–96 (Arabic); Peter Dodd and Halim Barakat, *River without Bridges: A Study of the Exodus of the 1967 Palestinian Arab Refugees* (Beirut: Institute for Palestine Studies, 1969).

12. Khalili, *Palestinian Women and the Revolution*, pp.89–93.

13. Khalili, *Ibid.*, p.14.

14. The Popular Front experienced much splintering during the Jordanian period, but its main competition came from the Democratic Front, which split in 1969. The Democratic Front was formed by those who wanted to adopt Marxism-Leninism as their ideology, which, at the time, was rejected by the Popular Front. Soon after, it did adopt Marxism-Leninism, but the ideological disagreement continued about who is the better Marxist-Leninist.

15. Abu Ali, *Introduction to Women's Reality and Their Experience in the Palestinian Revolution*, p. 158.

16. Abu Ali, *Ibid.*, p.70. For review of various factions' attitudes towards the women's questions, see pp.64–73.

17. Out of these concerns surfaced a series of articles in the Palestinian movement's media. The best of them is found in Khalili's *Palestinian Women and the Revolution*, pp.286–93. Khalili provided a number of items that focused on women in the movement during the period 1968–1975: *al-Hadaf*, voice of the Popular Front, had the most items (68); al-Saiqa's publication had 49; voice of the Popular Front-General Command's had 43; the Democratic Front's *al-Hurriya* had 41; and *Falastin al-Thawra*, of Fateh and the PLO had 34.

18. Under the democratization policies of Jordan, which began in 1989, three of the Palestinian fronts have now formed political parties. The Democratic Front-Nayef Hawatmeh operates under the name the Party of the Jordanian People; the party of the Democratic Front-Yasser Abed Rabbo operates under the name the Jordanian Democratic Party; and the Popular Front works under the name the Party of Jordanian Popular Unity. Fateh remains the only Palestinian faction that is not directly active in Jordanian party politics, conforming to the old agreement made with King Hussein not to interfere in internal Jordanian politics.

CHAPTER 3. BEIRUT: NATIONAL MOBILIZATION AND CIVIL WAR

1. Part of this chapter appeared as "National Mobilization, War Conditions, and Gender Consciousness," *Arab Studies Journal* 15(Spring, 1993): pp.53–67.

2. The popular committees contained men from the old camp leadership, such as village chiefs, plus representatives of the Resistance factions; some of the committees also had women.

3. For review, see Hussein Abu al-Ala', "The Camp: An Historical Reading," *Samed al-Iqtisadi* 13 (January/February/March, 1991): pp.109–125. (Arabic); and Yusuf Ma'adi, "Demographic, Economic, and Social Characteristics of Palestinians in Ein al-Hilwi Camp in Lebanon," *Ibid.*, pp.126–132.

4. Rex Brynen, *Sanctuary and Survival: The PLO in Lebanon* (Boulder: Westview Press, 1990), pp.46–48.

5. For review of Palestinian women's mobilization in Lebanon, see Julie Peteet, *Gender in Crisis: Women and the Palestinian Movement* (New York: Columbia University Press, 1991); Rosemary Sayigh, "Palestinian Women and Politics in Lebanon," in *Arab Women: Old Boundaries and New Frontiers*, edited by Judith Tucker (Bloomington: Indiana University Press, 1993), pp.175–192; and Khalili, *Palestinian Women and the Revolution*.

6. For a review of the activities of the branches of the PLO Women's Union, see Laurie Brand, *Palestinians in the Arab World: Institution Building and the Search for State* (New York: Columbia University Press, 1988).

7. According to Ghania Mulhis, an economist who was a member of Samed's executive committee in the late '70s, the foundation had thirty-three factories, mainly for clothing, fabrics, shoes, food, and furniture. Mulhis also said that 90 percent of the workforce was female. For a brief review of the PLO's social and economic institutions, see Brynen, *Sanctuary and Survival*, pp.140–141; and Ibrahim al-Jundi, "Samed Institution: The Experience of Twenty Years," *Samed al-Iqtisadi* 12 (January/February/March, 1990): pp.18–38. (Arabic).

8. Abu Ali, *Introduction to Women's Reality and Their Experience in the Palestinian Revolution*, pp.161–163.

9. Mai Sayigh, *The Siege* (Beirut: Arab Foundation for Research and Publication, 1988).

10. *Ibid.*, p. 264.

CHAPTER 4. TUNIS: DECLINE OF MOBILIZATION
IN THE PALESTINIAN DIASPORA

1. For accounts of the PLO schism, see *MERIP Reports*, special issue, 13(November/December, 1983); "DFLP-PFLP Joint Program of a

Comprehensive Reform within the PLO in the Political, Organizational, Military and Financial Fields, Damascus, October 16, 1983 (Excerpts)," *Journal of Palestine Studies* 3(Winter, 1984): pp.207–212; and Rex Brynen, *Sanctuary and Survival: The PLO in Lebanon* (Boulder: Westview Press, 1990), pp.184–93.

2. For a personal account from the War of the Camps, see Rosemary Sayigh, "The Third Siege of Bourj Barajneh Camp: A Woman's Testimony," *Race and Class* 29, 1(1987): pp.25–34. The various aspects of the Iron Fist policy are described in Joost Hiltermann, *Behind the Intifada: Labor and Women's Movements in the Occupied Territories* (Princeton: Princeton University Press, 1991).

3. The population of the Yarmuk Camp exceeded 50,000 and the total Palestinian population in Syria, according to UNRWA estimates, was 276,203 (1989).

4. The other was Faiza Yousuf, who was kept on as an independent after resigning from the Palestine Liberation Front, which she had represented in the secretariat.

5. Reuters Wire Service, July 10, 1985.

6. Another paragraph (307) did register concern for the situation of Palestinian women in Lebanon and in the Occupied Territories. The text of paragraphs 95 and 307 of the Forward-Looking Strategies can be found in "Documents and Source Material," *Journal of Palestine Studies* 14 (Summer, 1985): pp.188–189.

7. For a brief note of the PLO-French relationship, see "Can France Play a Useful Role in the Middle East?" *Journal of Palestine Studies* 15(Autumn, 1985): pp.189–190.

8. In the early 1990s, the Women's Union sent emissaries to start branches in London and New York, but that effort did not progress above the preparatory stage. Interestingly, Jihan Helou, who was a leader in Lebanon and who sided with Arafat's critics in 1983, presided over the preparatory conference in London, where she lived. The problem facing such initiatives has generally been lack of local organizing skills and little enthusiasm among the Palestinian women in these Western countries.

9. *Jordan Times*, September 29, 1991, p.1.

10. This was reported in Mohamed Rabie, "The U.S.-PLO Dialogue: The Swedish Connection," *Journal of Palestine Studies* 1, 21 (Summer, 1992): pp.54–66.

11. In the other points, the conferees declared that for the benefit of the two peoples the occupation must end (point two); that the Palestinians have the right to self-determination and sovereignty (point three); that all the people in the region have the right to live in freedom, dignity and security (point four); and that the purpose of the negotiations is to find a

just and permanent solution (point seven). (Source: Israel Women's Network Fax, October 18, 1993).

CHAPTER 5. JERUSALEM: WOMEN'S COMMITTEES IN THE OCCUPIED TERRITORIES

1. "Women's Day in the West Bank," *al-Fajr* March 14, 1984, pp. 8–9.

2. The PLO slate included the Palestine Communist Party which was not, at the time, represented in the PLO. The party officially joined the PLO at the 18th Palestine National Council session, held in 1987.

3. The National Guidance Committee was elected in 1978 at a national conference held in Jerusalem. The Israeli government cracked down on the Committee with arrests and deportations and it was formally banned in 1982. See Hiltermann, *Behind the Intifada: Labor and Women's Movements in the Occupied Territories*, pp.47–48.

4. There are over 200 charitable societies in the Occupied Territories, of which fifty are women's societies. They operate hospitals, medical clinics and rehabilitation centers, schools, orphanages, vocational centers and many other social welfare activities. Most are located in the West Bank and are community-based. Examples include: the Palestine Red Crescent, In'ash al-Usra of al-Bireh, al-Nahda Women's Society of Ramallah, Qalandia Camp Cooperative, Muslim Friends of the Orphanage Home/Jerusalem, Child Care Society of Beitjala, Young Women's Christian Society/Jerusalem, the Orthodox Bearers of the Cross/Jerusalem, and the Arab Women's Union/Ramallah. In the Gaza Strip are the Palestine Women's Union and Red Crescent Society/Gaza, and the Young Women's Muslim Association. For a complete listing, see Women's Studies' Committee of Bisan Center for Research and Development, *Directory of Palestinian Women's Organizations* (Jerusalem: Bisan Center for Research and Development and United Nations Development Programme, 1993).

5. In the 1970s, six Palestinian universities were established: Birzeit (that grew from a secondary school and a junior college), Bethlehem, al-Najah, and Jerusalem universities in the West Bank and Gaza Islamic University in the Gaza Strip. The number of women attending higher education rose until the Intifada, when it declined. For additional review, see Gabi Baramki, "Building Palestinian Universities Under Occupation," *Journal of Palestine Studies* 27(Autumn 1987): pp.12–20; Amal Khriesheh, "The Palestinian Woman and Work," *Shuun Tanmawiyah* (December 1988): pp.13–14. (Arabic); and Zahira Kamal, "Development of the Palestinian Women's Movement," *darb al-mar'a* (April 1987). (Arabic).

6. There was also a fifth group that came about in the late 1980s, the Ba'athist Women's Struggle Committees, but it was very small and its members were active mainly in some of the societies and social clubs.

7. The third generation received their undergraduate education mainly at Birzeit University and the University of Jordan.

8. Marianne Heiberg and Geir Ovensen, *Palestinian Society in Gaza, West Bank and Arab Jerusalem: A Survey of Living Conditions* (Oslo: Fagbevegelsens Senter for Forskning, 1993), pp.40–42.

9. Intissar Azmi, "Gaza Strip Camps: An History of Suffering and Resistance to the Occupation," *Samed al-Iqtisadi* 13(January/February/March, 1991): pp.38–54. (Arabic); and Heiberg and Ovensen, *Palestinian Society in Gaza, West Bank and Arab Jerusalem: A Survey of Living Conditions*, pp.40–42.

10. The *Journal of Palestine Studies* is one of the best sources of articles about the Palestinian economy in the Occupied Territories. See, for example, Yusif Sayigh, "The Palestinian Economy Under Occupation," 15(Summer, 1986): pp.46–67; Sara Roy, "The Gaza Strip: A Case of Economic De-Development," 17(Autumn, 1987): pp.56–88; Rami Abdul-hadi, "Land Use Planning in the Occupied Territories," 19(Summer, 1990): pp.46–63; and Sara Roy, "Gaza: New Dynamics of Civic Disintegration," 22(Summer, 1993): pp.20–31.

11. For review of the rise of Hamas and other Islamic groups in the Gaza Strip, see Ziad Abu-Amr, *Islamic Fundamentalism in the West Bank and Gaza* (Bloomington: Indiana University Press, 1994). See also "Charter of the Islamic Resistance Movement (HAMAS) of Palestine," *Journal of Palestine Studies* 22(Summer, 1993): pp.122–134.

12. Overall, in 1987, 24.4 percent of females and 34.2 percent of males in the West Bank completed 9–12 years of schooling; in the Gaza Strip, the numbers were 37.1 percent of females and 39.8 percent of males. Among the 15–17 year age group, the numbers rise, for example, in the West Bank, 55.2 percent of females and 62.2 percent of males finished 9–12 years of schooling. Among females aged 25–44 years—the age group of most housewives—an average of 18.5 percent in the West Bank and 38.8 percent in the Gaza Strip finished 9–12 years of schooling. Over three-fourths of women forty-five and older in the Occupied Territories have had no formal education at all. The statistics indicate that, generally, the level of secondary and college education rose steadily for both males and females, but more so among the latter. (Source: Statistical Abstracts of Israel 1988, No. 39. Table XVII/46. Jerusalem: Central Bureau of Statistics.)

13. For additional statistics from the '70s, see Elias H. Tuma and Haim Darin-Drabkin, *The Economic Case for Palestine* (London: Croom Helm, 1978), pp.47–49, 72, 100.

14. The Middle Camps refers to Breij, Marazi, Nuseirat, and Deir al-Balah refugee camps, and the villages of Deir al-Balah and al-Zawaj.

15. The use of foreign donors, observed Sara Roy, helped the various groups become more autonomous from the PLO, in Sara Roy, "Gaza: New Dynamics of Civic Disintegration," *Journal of Palestine Studies*, pp.20–31.

16. For a review of the labor movement in the Occupied Territories, see Hiltermann, *Behind the Intifada*, pp.56–125.

17. Unified National Leadership of the Uprising communiques, numbers eight and nine.

18. According to Islah Jad, only guard duties were solely performed by males, in Islah Jad, "From Salons to the Popular Committees: Palestinian Women, 1919–1989," in *Palestine Intifada at the Crossroads*, edited by Jamal Nassar and Roger Hickocks (New York: Praeger, 1989), pp.125–141.

19. The information provided here on Islamic fundamentalism is mainly found in Ziad Abu-Amr, *Islamic Fundamentalism in the West Bank and Gaza* (Bloomington: Indiana University Press, 1994).

20. See "Charter of the Islamic Resistance Movement (HAMAS) of Palestine," *Journal of Palestine Studies*, pp.122–127.

21. Colors are important political symbols in the Occupied Territories: The 1948 border that separates the territories from Israel is called the Green Line; the color of identity cards changes as one crosses that line and so does the color of car license plates—for example, a green license plate indicates that the car belongs to a Palestinian from the West Bank. And then there are the ultimate symbols of the two nations: the Israeli blue and white and the Palestinian red, green, white, and black. The Intifada graffiti always used the Palestinian colors, with each group identified with certain ones. Hamas' graffiti was drawn in green and black, the colors of Islam.

22. "Results of Palestinian Public Opinion About the Elections, the Economic Situation, the (Palestinian) Police, the Palestinian Prisoners, and the City of Jerusalem," *al-Quds*, July 14, 1994, pp.16–17. (Arabic).

23. "Charter of the Islamic Resistance Movement (HAMAS) of Palestine," *Journal of Palestine Studies*, p.128.

24. Support of the Popular Front and other leftist groups varies throughout the West Bank and Gaza Strip and does approach a combined 20 percent in some locations. See "Results of Palestinian Public Opinion," *al-Quds*, p. 17.

25. Similar encounters were noted by Rema Hammami in her "Women's Participation in the Intifada, A Critical Overview," in *The Intifada and Some Women's Social Issues, Proceedings of a Conference Held in Al-Quds Al-Sharif/ Jerusalem on December 14, 1990*, prepared by the

Women's Studies' Committee/ Bisan Center for Research and Development, pp.73–83.

26. Quoted in *Ibid.*, p.80.

27. In the aftermath of the break-up, Kamal's union changed its focus from extensive outreach to building model projects (the first was a women's counseling center, which opened in Jerusalem in 1992). By 1994, however, the group, under its new head Siham Barghouti, had truly moved to decentralize, having urged its members in the various localities to form their own women's action societies and to raise their own funds.

28. Sara Roy also observed a decline in the use of the veil during her visit in 1993, in her "Gaza: New Dynamics of Civic Disintegration," *Journal of Palestine Studies*, p.23.

29. Until now, the West Bank used the Jordanian personal status law, while the Gaza Strip is under the Egyptian rules. In reality, because of the political situation, implementation has been very difficult. Shaykh Abdel Hamid Sayeh, a known liberal cleric who was also president of the Palestine National Council, said that personal status law in the Gaza Strip is based on Egypt's and, in the West Bank, on Jordanian law. In our interview in 1990, Sayeh predicted that the Palestinian law would be patterned on one or the other systems.

30. For a short while, in 1992, Rouda Basiir from Nablus, West Bank, led the Women's Action Union.

31. The Popular Front's opposition to Um Jihad's leadership resurfaced later in August, when Maha Nassar, the Front's top woman, objected to Um Jihad taking a leading role at the planned conference of the West Bank branch of the General Union of Palestinian Women. Consequently, the conference was delayed until the matter was resolved.

32. Marianne Heiberg and Geir Ovensen, *Palestinian Society in Gaza, West Bank and Arab Jerusalem: A Survey of Living Conditions* (Oslo: Fagbevegelsens Senter for Forskning, 1993), pp.249–282.

EPILOGUE

1. In Elia Zureik, "Palestinian Refugees and Peace," *Journal of Palestine Studies* 25(Autumn, 1994): p.6.

2. In Maxine Molyneux, "Mobilization Without Emancipation? Women's Interests, State, and Revolution," pp.280–302, in Richard R. Fagen, Carmen Diana Deere, and Jose Luis Coraggio *Transition and Development: Problems of Third World Socialism* (Boston: Monthly Review Press, 1986).

REFERENCES

Abdel Haq, Yussef. "Social Security in the Palestinian Struggle," *Samed al-Iqtisadi* 12(January/February/March, 1990): pp.39–49. (Arabic).

Abdel Nasser, Gamal. *Collection of Speeches, Announcements, and Declarations of the President.* Volumes I–IV, July 23, 1952–June, 1964 (Cairo: UAR Information Service, 1964). (Arabic).

Abdulhadi, Rami. "Land Use Planning in the Occupied Territories," *Journal of Palestine Studies* 19(Summer 1990): pp.46–63.

Abu al-Ala', Hussein. "The Camp: An Historical Reading," *Samed al-Iqtisadi* 13(January/February/March, 1991): pp.109–125. (Arabic).

Abu Ali, Khadijeh. *Introduction to Women's Reality and Their Experience in the Palestinian Revolution.* Beirut: General Union of Palestinian Women, 1975. (Arabic).

———. "The Political Role of Palestinian Women on the International Level," *Samed al-Iqtisadi* 8(1986): pp.91–109. (Arabic).

Abu-Amr, Ziad. *Islamic Fundamentalism in the West Bank and Gaza.* (Bloomington: Indiana University Press, 1994).

Abu Iyad. (nom de guerre of Salah Khalaf, with Eric Rouleau), *My Home, My Land: A Narrative of the Palestinian Struggle.* (New York: Times Books, 1981).

Ahmad, Wedad. *Palestinian Women and the Intifada.* Tunis: General Union of Palestinian Women, 1988. (Arabic).

Aruri, Nasser H. and Samih Farsoun. "Palestinian Communities and Arab Host Countries," In *The Sociology of the Palestinians*, Khalil Nakhleh and Elia Zureik, eds. (New York: St. Martin's Press, 1980).

Azmi, Intissar. "Gaza Strip Camps: An History of Suffering and Resistance to the Occupation," *Samed al-Iqtisadi* 13(January/February/March, 1991): pp.38–54. (Arabic).

Badran, Margot and Miriam Cooke, eds. *Opening the Gates.* (Bloomington: Indiana University Press, 1990).

Baramki, Gabi. "Building Palestinian Universities Under Occupation," *Journal of Palestine Studies* 27(Autumn, 1987): pp.12–20.

Brand, Laurie. *Palestinians in the Arab World: Institution Building and the Search for State.* (New York: Columbia University Press, 1988).

Brynen, Rex. *Sanctuary and Survival: the PLO in Lebanon.* (Boulder: Westview Press, 1990).

"Can France Play a Useful Role in the Middle East?" *Journal of Palestine Studies* 15(Autumn, 1985): pp.189–190.

"Charter of the Islamic Resistance Movement (HAMAS) of Palestine." *Journal of Palestine Studies* 22(Summer, 1993): pp.122–134.

Che-Guevara, Ernesto. *Guerrilla de Guerrillas in Obra Revolucianaria.* (Mexico: Ediciones Era Mexico, D.F., 1967).

"DFLP-PFLP Joint Program of a Comprehensive Reform within the PLO in the Political, Organizational, Military and Financial Fields," Damascus, October 16, 1983, (Excerpts). *Journal of Palestine Studies* 13(Winter, 1984): pp.207–212.

"Documents and Source Material," *Journal of Palestine Studies* 14 (Summer, 1985): pp.188–189.

Dodd, Peter and Halim Barakat. *River without Bridges: A Study of the Exodus of the 1967 Palestinian Arab Refugees.* (Beirut: Institute for Palestine Studies, 1969).

Fernea, Elizabeth Warnock ed. *Women and the Family in the Middle East.* (Austin: University of Texas Press, 1985).

Fromkin, David. *A Peace to End All Peace.* (New York: Henry Holt and Co., 1989).

Giap, General Yu Nguyen. *The People's War and the People's Army.* (Hanoi: Foreign Languages Press, 1961).

Hammami, Rema. "Women's Participation in the Intifada, A Critical Overview," pp.73–83. In *The Intifada and Some Women's Social Issues: Proceedings of a Conference Held in Al-Quds Al-Sharif/ Jerusalem on December 14, 1990,* prepared by the Women's Studies Committee/Bisan Center for Research and Development.

Hart, Alan. *Arafat: A Political Biography.* (Bloomington: Indiana University Press, 1984).

Heiberg, Marianne and Geir Ovensen. *Palestinian Society in Gaza, West Bank and Arab Jerusalem.* (Oslo: Fagbevegelsens Senter for Forskning, 1993).

Hiltermann, Joost. *Behind the Intifada: Labor and Women's Movements in the Occupied Territories.* (Princeton: Princeton University Press, 1991).

Jammal, Laila. *Contributions by Palestinian Women to the National Struqqle for Liberation.* (Washington, D.C.: Middle East Public Relations, 1985).

Jankowski, James. "Egyptian Responses to the Palestine Problem in the Interwar Period," *International Journal of Middle Eastern Studies* 12(1980): pp.1–38.

Jordan Times, September 29, 1991.

Al-Jundi, Ibrahim. "Samed Institution: The Experience of Twenty Years," *Samed al-Iqtisadi* 12(January/February/March, 1990): pp.18–38. (Arabic).

Kamal, Zahira. "Development of Palestinian Women's Movement," *darb al-mar'a* (April, 1987). (Single Issue). (Arabic).

Kawar, Amal. "National Mobilization, War Conditions, and Gender Consciousness," *Arab Studies Quarterly* 15(Spring, 1993): pp.53–67.

Khalifa, Sahar, Islah Jad, and Rita Giacaman. *Women's Affairs*. (May, 1991). (Nablus, West Bank: Women's Affairs Society). (Arabic).

Khalili, Ghazi. *Palestinian Women and the Revolution*. (Beirut: Palestine Liberation Organization, 1977). (Arabic).

Khriesheh, Amal. "Palestinian Women and Work," *Shuun Tanmawiyah* (December, 1988): pp.13–14. (Arabic).

Lockman, Zachary and Joel Beinin. *Intifada: The Palestinian Uprising Against Israeli Occupation*. A MERIP Book. (Boston: South End Press, 1989).

Ma'adi, Yusuf. "Demographic, Economic, and Social Characteristics of Palestinians in Ein al-Hilwi Camp in Lebanon," *Samed al-Iqtisadi* 13(January/February/March, 1991): pp.126–132. (Arabic).

Mansi, Kamel. "The Palestinian Refugee Camps in Jordan," *Samed al-Iqtisadi* 13(January/February/March, 1991): pp.79–96. (Arabic).

Mao Tse-tung. *Selected Writings*. (Beijing: Foreign Languages Press, 1961 and 1965).

MERIP Reports. (Special issue). 13(November/December, 1983).

Mernissi, Fatima. *Beyond the Veil: Male-Female Dynamics in Modern Muslim Society*. (Bloomington: Indiana University Press, 1987).

Mogannam, Matiel E.T. *The Arab Woman: and the Palestine Problem*. (Westport, Conn.: Hyperion Press, Inc., 1976). (Reprint of 1937 Arabic version).

Molyneux, Maxine. "Mobilization without Emancipation? Women's Interests, State, and Revolution," pp.280–302 in *Transition and Development: Problems of Third World Socialism*. Richard R. Fagen, Diana Deere, and Jose Luis Coraggio, eds. (Boston: Monthly Review Press, 1986).

Morgan, Robin, ed. *Sisterhood Is Global*. (Garden City, N.Y.: Anchor Press/Doubleday, 1984).

Musallam, Sami. *The Palestine Liberation Organization: Its Functions and Structure*. (Brattleboro, Vt.: Amana Books, 1988).

Nahid, Toubia, ed. *Women of the Arab World: The Coming Challenge.* (London: Zed Books Ltd., 1988).

Najjar, Orayb. *Portraits of Palestinian Women.* (Salt Lake City, University of Utah Press, 1992).

Nakhleh, Khalil and Elia Zureik, eds. *The Sociology of the Palestinians.* (New York: St. Martin's Press, 1980).

Nassar, Jamal and Roger Hickocks, eds. *Palestine Intifada at the Crossroads.* (New York: Praeger, 1989).

Nelson, Cynthia. "Public and Private Politics: Women in the Middle Eastern World," *American Ethnologist.* 1,3(1974): pp.551–563.

Palestine Liberation Organization. *Report of the Palestine National Council's Nineteenth Session, October 12–15, 1988.* (Arabic).

Palestinian Leaders Discuss the New Challenges for the Resistance. Political Essays, No. 42 (Beirut: Palestine Research Center, 1974).

Peteet, Julie M. *Gender in Crisis: Women and the Palestinian Resistance Movement.* (New York: Columbia University Press, 1991).

Popular Front for the Liberation of Palestine. *Political Report of the PFLP's Fourth Congress.* (Damascus: PFLP Central Information Committee, 1986). (Arabic).

Rabie, Mohamed. "The U.S.-PLO Dialogue: The Swedish Connection," *Journal of Palestine Studies* 21(Summer, 1992): pp.54–66.

Rashmawi, Muna. *Preliminaries Concerning Palestinian Women in Historical Experience and the Law.* (Ramallah, West Bank: Law in the Service of Man). (Arabic).

"Results of Palestinian Public Opinion About the Elections, the Economic Situation, the (Palestinian) Police, the Palestinian Prisoners, and the City of Jerusalem," *al-Quds* July 7, 1994: pp.16–17. (Arabic).

Ridd, Rosemary and Helen Callaway, eds. *Women and Political Conflict: Portraits of Struggle in Times of Crisis.* (New York: New York University Press, 1987).

Rigby, Andrew. *Living the Intifada.* (London: Zed Books Ltd., 1991).

Rosenwasser, Penny. *Voices from a "Promised Land": Palestinian and Israeli Peace Activists Speak their Hearts.* (Williamantic, Conn.: Curbstone Press, 1992).

Roy, Sara. "Gaza: New Dynamics of Civic Disintegration," *Journal of Palestine Studies* 22(Summer, 1993): pp.20–31.

———. "The Gaza Strip: A Case of Economic De-Development," *Journal of Palestine Studies* 17(Autumn, 1987): pp.56–88.

Sabbagh, Suha. "Interview: Yasser Arafat on the Role of Palestinian Women," *The Return* 3(1990): pp.9–13.

Sayigh, Mai. *The Siege.* (Beirut: Arab Foundation for Research and Publication, 1988). (Arabic).

Sayigh, Rosemary. *Palestinians: From Peasants to Revolutionaries.* (London: Zed Press, 1979).

———. "Encounters with Palestinian Women Under Occupation," *Journal of Palestine Studies.* 10(Summer, 1981): pp.3–26.

———. The Third Siege of Bourj Barajneh Camp: A Woman's Testimony," *Race and Class.* 29,1(1987): pp.25–34.

Sayigh, Yusif. "The Palestinian Economy Under Occupation," *Journal of Palestine Studies* 15(Summer, 1986): pp.46–67.

Sharabi, Hisham. *Palestine Guerrillas: Their Credibility and Effectiveness.* Monographs Series, No. 25. (Beirut: The Institute for Palestine Studies, 1970).

Shlaim, Avi. "The Rise and Fall of the All-Palestine Government in Gaza," *Journal of Palestine Studies* 20(Autumn, 1990): pp.37–53.

Smith, Jane. *Women and Contemporary Muslim Societies.* (Lewisburg: Bucknell University Press, 1980).

Statistical Abstracts of Israel. No. 39. Table XVII/46 (Jerusalem: Central Bureau of Statistics, 1988).

Strum, Philippa. *The Women are Marching: The Second Sex and the Palestinian Revolution.* (Brooklyn, N.Y.: Lawrence Hill Books, 1992).

Talhami, Ghada. "Women in the Movement: Their Long, Uncelebrated History," *Al-Fajr,* May 20, 1986: pp.8–9.

Tawil, Raymonda Hawa. *My Home, My Prison.* (London: Zed Books Ltd.,1983).

Toubia, Nahid, ed. *Women of the Arab World.* (London: Zed Books Ltd., 1988).

Tucker, Judy, ed. *Arab Women: Old Boundaries and New Frontiers.* (Bloomington: Indiana University Press, 1993).

Tuma, Elias H. and Haim Darin-Drabkin. *The Economic Case for Palestine.* (London: Croom Helm, 1978).

Turki, Fawaz. *The Disinherited.* (New York: Monthly Review Press, 1972).

UNESCO. *Social Science Research and Women in the Arab World.* (London: Frances Pinter Publishers, 1984).

Al-Wahidi, Maisoun. *Arab Women in Palestine.* (Tunis: General Secretariat, General Administration for Social and Cultural Affairs, Administration of Women's and Family Affairs, 1985). (Arabic).

Waines, David. "Through a Veil Darkly: The Study of Women in Muslim Societies," *Comparative Studies in Society and History.* 24(1982): pp.642–659.

Warnock, Kitty. *Land Before Honour: Palestinian Women in the Occupied Territories.* (New York: Monthly Review Press, 1990).

"Women in an Islamic Palestine," *The Economist* September 17, 1994: pp.41–42.

"Women's Day in the West Bank," *al-Fajr* March 14, 1984, pp.8–9.

Women's PACKET: A Collection of Database Project Documentation on Women and the Palestinian Uprising. (Chicago: The Database Project on Palestinian Human Rights, 1990).

Women's Studies Committee of Bisan Center for Research and Development. *Directory of Palestinian Women's Organizations.* (Bisan Center for Research and Development and United Nations Development Programme, 1993).

Zureik, Elia. "Palestinian Refugees and Peace," *Journal of Palestine Studies* 25(Autumn, 1994): pp.5–17.

INDEX